D1276015

ıors

Marius Leibold

is a Business Consultant in Innovation & Strategy Management, and Professor in Strategy at Stellenbosch University
and at the Netherlands Business School. His research focuses on new business models and innovation for global
competitiveness, incorporating strategic fitness, systemic
innovation and talent management approaches applied in
ıdustries and companies. He is author of several managerial books
us articles on innovation and strategy, and is a Director of the
gram, a collaborative research program between academic and
organizations in the USA, Europe, Africa and Asia. He advises
irectors and executives on innovative business models responding
ological, societal and economic trends.

e contacted at: ml@leibold.cc

Sven C. Voelpel

is the Director of the research group WISE (for Wisdom - Innovation - Strategy - Energy) and Professor of Business Administration at the Jacobs Center for Lifelong Learning and
Institutional Development of the International University
Bremen (IUB), Germany. His research explores these fields
of Wisdom, Innovation, Strategy and Energy and has con-
l to these domains, including Change Management and Knowledge
ement, with more than 100 publications in books and journals. His
ecent book (co-authored with Thomas Davenport and Marius Lei-
Strategic Management in the Innovation Economy (Wiley, 2006).
tly Professor Voelpel is working on business models, strategies for
l and sustainability in the changing workforce arenas with particu-
cusing on solutions for Managing the Aging Workforce. He has been
with various (honorary) professorships around the globe, and as a
Fellow at Harvard University.

be contacted at: s.voelpel@iu-bremen.de

The auth

Ma

various i
and vari
WISE pr
business
CEO's, c
to techn
He can h

tribute
Manag
most
bold)
Curre
surviv
larly f
servin
Visiti
He ca

Managing the Aging Workforce

Challenges and Solutions

by Marius Leibold
and Sven Voelpel

Bibliographic information published by Die Deutsche Nationalbibliothek
Die Deutsche Nationalbibliothek lists this publication in the Deutsche
Nationalbibliografie; detailed bibliographic data is available in the Internet
at http://dnb.d-nb.de.

www.publicis-erlangen.de/books
www.wiley-vch.de
www.wiley.com

ISBN-13: 978-3-89578-284-8
ISBN-10: 3-89578-284-X

A joint publication of Publicis Corporate Publishing and
Wiley-VCH-Verlag GmbH & Co KGaA
© 2006 by Publicis KommunikationsAgentur GmbH, GWA, Erlangen

Printed in Germany

The world is facing an unprecedented war for talent and competencies. Will your company be able to manage this and survive? Here is what others say:

"The rapidly aging global workforce is considered by many to be the most significant business and societal trend for the next several decades."

Lorrie Foster, *The Conference Board*

"Going grey with worry: Ex-communist countries risk growing old before they become rich."

'Demography in Eastern Europe,'
The Economist, May 27, 2006, p. 48

"Dramatic trends are already in motion that will force organizations to do some major rethinking about their relationships with their employees."

Harriet Hankin, *The New Workforce: Five Sweeping Trends that will Shape Your Company's Future.*

"... the problems are bigger than we imagine. We have never had such an older age mix in the workforce or a generation as large as the baby boomers preparing to retire."

Ken Dychtwald, Tamara Erickson & Robert Morison, *Workforce Crisis*

"In the developed countries, the dominant factor in the 21st century will be the rapid growth in the older population and the rapid shrinking of the younger generation."

Peter Drucker

Prologues

Critical Workforce Solutions for Leaders and Managers

Many countries in the world, including Germany, Japan, the U.S. and even China, are facing a crisis during the first decade of the 21st century and beyond: the aging of the their populations due to declining birthrates, longer life-spans of people, the retirement wave of Baby Boomers now reaching age 60 from 2006 onward, and the demands of the global economy for creative human resources for innovation.

This crisis impacts several levels, such as social (pension-fund demands, financing escalating social benefits), economic (global competitiveness increasingly depends on innovation), industry (rising human resource costs), and enterprise (competition for talent, preventing loss of key knowledge).

Several publications have recently appeared that alert decision-makers about the impending crisis and its critical challenges. This book goes an important step further – it provides approaches and solutions from business leaders and managers that are aimed specifically at the aging workforce. It is the first publication that provides an overview of both challenges and solutions for enterprises, as well as an integrated scorecard tool for five of the key managerial areas concerning an aging workforce.

The key contribution of this book is its renewed focus on how to utilize aging employees better and longer in enterprises. The emphasis on life-long learning, aging worker-sensitive environments, new cooperative approaches with trade unions, and health challenges – mental and emotional – of aging employees, all point to a new role for human resource management in enterprises – one that emphasizes an aging workforce need and requirements. It is important to realize that this is not a choice for leaders and managers, but an absolute necessity for survival.

I am pleased to provide this foreword, and I recommend that managers read the book and apply its advice urgently and wisely. I congratulate the authors and the Jacobs Center for Life-Long Learning at International University of Bremen for their initiative. I trust it will stimulate even more guides and tools for leaders and managers designed to help us in addressing the crisis of workforce aging and its impacts on all levels of society.

Heinrich von Pierer,
Chairman of the Supervisory Board, Siemens AG

Aging Human Capital and the New Role of HR Management

Demographic changes and globalization are among the most important challenges of the future. The younger and middle-aged populations of Western societies decrease, whereas the older population increases in size. One of the main results is a skills shortage entailing a global 'war for talents' in a business world primarily characterized by a concurrent cost, productivity, and quality pressures.

There is an increasing awareness about the implications of demographic changes influencing organizational human capital policies and procedures. Although human capital issues with a short- and medium-term impact still take precedence over long-term considerations and strategies, and the immediate pressure induced by the demographic development appears to be comparably low, many organizations start seeking solutions to encounter the risks and also to benefit from an experienced aging workforce.

This book addresses challenges as well as solutions based upon the value-add of an aging human capital in a 'brave new world of work'. It meets the need for a multi-dimensional, integrated, comprehensive, and dynamic approach, incorporating research results across various disciplines such as business administration, neuroscience, education, sociology, psychology, and communications. The authors emphasize quite clearly that all organizational activities and initiatives should be closely linked and intertwined in order to be successful and sustainable.

Soft and hard facts, qualitative and quantitative issues as well as the most critical fields of activity with regards to an aging workforce are thoroughly explored, structured, and presented. This framework helps organizations answer some of the most important questions: What are the implications and costs of an aging workforce? What is the return on investment of any change, knowledge, health, and human resources management initiatives? What is the impact upon leadership and corporate culture?

The overall objective of an organization is to maintain and increase creativity and innovative power, work ability and productivity in order to keep its competitive edge in a global market with and not despite an aging workforce. The ability to positively and proactively anticipate the challenges of the demographic changes and to use the current age structure of the organization, the industry, or even the country for productivity, innovation, and competitive advantage is what we call 'demographic fitness'.

This complex challenge also needs a newly defined, extended role of HR service providers, who will have to know much about the aging workforce's needs and desires to make their enterprises fit for global future.

This book will assist you as leaders, managers, and employees to face and embrace the challenges, to jointly create innovative and sustainable solutions, and to eventually achieve organizational demographic fitness today and in the future.

Klaus J. Jacobs,
Chairman Adecco Group

Contents

PART I   The Challenge Ahead

PART II Managerial Objectives

PART III   The Five Value-Adding Fields

PART IV Putting It All Together

Introduction

Businesses in developed countries worldwide are facing a critical challenge: managing an aging (and declining) skilled workforce. Executives today are waking up to the realization that their firms will encounter a wave of retirements over the next decade as the 'baby boomers' of the post-World War II era reach retirement age. At the other end of the talent pipeline, birthrates have been declining significantly over the past 20 years, with the pool of new talent shrinking, and the younger workforce is also developing a different set of work values and expectations than previous generations. Although these trends are especially evident in developed, industrialized countries, all countries worldwide are affected – the imminent 'war for talent' will also be affecting developing countries – as they will be facing shortages of skilled workers being drawn to developed countries – while developed countries will battle to retain a skilled, competitive workforce due to the large number of retirees.

To manage the aging workforce, leaders must have an accurate understanding of its current and shifting composition, likely impacts on different types of enterprises – and especially their own – and the strategic and operational approaches to use to ensure both innovative capability and effective operations. The main issues necessary to address are new leadership mindsets about the right business models in an aging society, new concepts in workforce health management – acquiring, utilizing, retaining, energizing and rejuvenating knowledge for innovation – and organizational learning, changing physical work environments, new ways of managing human resources, and new techniques to measure performance of an aging workforce.

Managing the Aging Workforce provides these new concepts and practical managerial approaches in four parts:

- Part I (Chapters 1 and 2) provides an understanding of the critical challenges of an aging society for an enterprise's workforce, and indicates how demographic trends will impact particular economies, industries and organizations. Questions such as why these challenges are crucial right now, and if these challenges can be managed, are addressed. Although the focus is on enterprises, the impacts for industries and economies are also indicated.

- Part II (Chapters 3 and 4) traces the nature of the changing value of workers for the 21st century enterprise, states the necessity for clear objectives in critical managerial areas, and presents the concept of a workforce scorecard tool – the 5V-framework (five critical aging workforce arenas) to manage (enable, guide and measure) both creativity and productivity of an enterprise's aging workforce.

- Part III consists of five chapters (Chapters 5 to 9), providing guidelines and approaches for each of five critical aging workforce arenas: mindset-changing approaches concerning an aging workforce in global demand and supply chains; knowledge management and organizational learning approaches; new health management approaches; new physical work environment approaches; and new human resource management approaches for the aging workforce. In chapters 5 and 6, particular misconceptions and myths of the aging workforce are highlighted and dispelled, and a practical knowledge management model for an aging workforce is proposed, with recommendations how to retain and even recover critical knowledge, and how to transfer tacit knowledge and 'deep smarts' of an aging workforce. Chapter 7 emphasizes that health is more than just a physical issue, and that it includes mental and emotional health. Integrated health management approaches for an aging workforce are proposed. In chapter 8 the right work environment platforms, processes and measures for an aging workforce are highlighted, and in chapter 9 appropriate human resources approaches and strategies for an aging workforce are outlined.

- Part IV provides (in Chapter 10) the integrated 5V-Scorecard for managing the aging workforce, and outlines the key integrated requirements for sustainably implementing and guiding the management of an enterprise's aging workforce. The dynamics of utilizing the 5V-Scorecard as an integrated system are illustrated.

Some of the facts outlined in this book may appear in more than one chapter. This is due to the fact that the aspects of managing the aging workforce are tied up among each other, and each of the chapters shall be readable on its own.

This is a solutions-oriented book with the purpose to assist 21st century enterprises in dealing with one of the most pressing management problems of the immediate coming years: how to sustain an enterprise in being continually innovative, effective and efficient in the coming 'war for talent'. The world is facing an unprecedented brain drain and those enterprise leaders adroitly managing the aging workforce – in their organizations and value chains – will emerge as the winners of the future.

This book became a reality due to stimulating ideas, comprehensive research, and intensive networking among many people. These include managers and executives in many enterprises, colleagues at International University Bremen, Harvard Business School, MIT Sloan Management School, and Stellenbosch University, as well as our students and research fellows. We are extraordinarily thankful that we have been able to work in the interdisciplinary context of the Jacobs Center for Lifelong Learning and Institutional Development (JCLL) at the International University Bremen (IUB), Sven Voelpel as the centre's Professor of Business Administration and Marius Leibold during his visits beyond the intensive virtual contacts.

The JCLL enabled us to address the topic of an aging workforce from a wider integrated perspective rooted in basic research of several disciplines. Various sessions to further establish the newly founded trans-disciplinary JCLL in 2003 as the world's hub institute on the mega-trend of lifelong learning and the aging workforce, countless faculty meetings for developing joint curricula, executive programs and above all joint research projects on this topic during more than two years, enabled us to understand the topic from a wider perspective. Therefore we would like to thank Dean Ursula Staudinger for her extraordinary commitment for establishing the JCLL and her and our JCLL faculty colleagues shared time: Ute Kunzmann and Britta Renner, with Ursula Staudinger our Professors of Psychology; Klaus Schömann, Professor of Sociology; Clemens Schwender, Professor of Communication Science; Benjamin Godde, Professor of Neuroscience and Human Performance as well as Dr. Claudia Voelcker-Rehage, Postdoctoral Fellow for Human Performance, especially also for her literature suggestions for the chapters on health management and work environment.

We are also thankful for JCLL's research associates, doctoral students and invited external scholars to share their experiences in various fields and leading expert speakers in our meetings, weekly seminars, Distinguished Lecture Series and JCLL Colloquium Series.

We also particularly thank Klaus J. Jacobs, in his capacity as the chairman of the board of the Jacobs Foundation and the Jacobs Foundation for the noble funding of the JCLL. Moreover we acknowledge the visionary foresight of Klaus Jacobs, in his recent function as Chairman & CEO of Adecco, the worldwide leader in Human Resource services, for strongly supporting our Executive Master Program in Lifelong Learning, Knowledge Management, and Institutional Change (LKI) that enabled us to exclusively train the Aging Workforce Consultants for this equally named newly established Adecco unit. This enabled us to develop curricula and to work for establishing practical concepts for companies with a very fast pace.

We are for this book particularly indebted to our research assistants Polina Isichenko, Chris Streb and Eden Tekie for their inputs, expert technical reviews of draft chapters by Maike Wilpert, and word-processing by Hanneke du Preez. Special thanks to our publisher Dr Gerhard Seitfudem for his motivation, support and professional editorial guidance.

Marius Leibold   Sven Voelpel

PART I

The Challenge Ahead

1 Critical Challenges of the Aging Workforce for Enterprise Sustainability and Survival

Key Issues of this Chapter

- How big and serious are these challenges?
- Why are they critical right now?
- What companies are responding to the challenges?
- Can the challenges be managed?
- What are the solutions for my company?

How Big and Serious are the Challenges of an Aging Workforce?

Brainpower, human competencies and physical energies are the very air that businesses breathe in the knowledge-networked global innovation economy of the early 21st century. In today's world, innovation capability and sustainable human endeavor are the essence of competitive survival and corporate sustainability. This is well realized by most enterprises, but what is surprisingly little appreciated is the looming impact of the aging workforce in the developed world on their sustained competitiveness and the growing of shareholder value.

The developed world's workforce – the key source for innovation and effective competencies – is shrinking at a frightening rate. Consider the evidence in a number of countries: in the United States, labor shortfalls of 5 to 10 million workers are expected in the next ten years[1] (see Figure 1.1); while a shortage of nearly one million workers in Canada is predicted over the next 20 years.[2] In the European Union (EU), populations are already decreasing in major countries, including Germany, France, Italy and Austria – and an influx of about one million immigrants a year into the EU is considered necessary to make up the shortfall in workers.[3] In Asia, Japan's birthrate continues to fall, with the number of workers of ages 35 to 44 predicted to shrink by 10% as early as 2010, while in China the similar type of workers is expected to shrink in number by 8% by 2010.[4]

The seriousness of this challenge is mirrored in the simple fact that by 2010, the number of 35 to 44 year olds that are normally expected to move into senior management ranks, will not grow but significantly decline – by 19% in the U.S., 27% in Germany, 19% in the U.K., 9% in Italy, and respectively 10% and 8% in Japan and China. Conversely, the number of aging workers will increase substantially, e.g. in the U.S. the workers aged 45 to 54 will grow by 21%, and the number of 55 to 64 year olds will grow by a whopping 52%.[5]

As a result of these dramatic demographic changes, global competition for skilled workers and creative talent is gradually increasing. Many countries and companies are starting to recognize the changing value of their aging workers, and the critical importance to retain, nurture and rejuvenate the value-adding contributions of the aging workforce. Some observers call it the 'com-

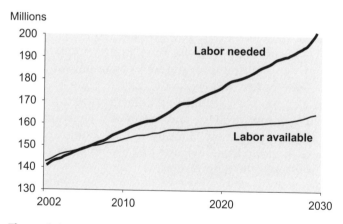

Figure 1.1
How labor demand will outstrip supply up to 2030
(Source: Employment Policy Foundation analysis and projections of Census/BLS and BEA data, *American Workplace Report 2002*)

ing world brain drain', an impending 'war for talent', and a 'workforce crisis'.[6]

Why are the Challenges Critical Right Now?

The challenges of a shrinking and aging workforce are critical right now, because enterprises are simply not geared to handle the convergence of four major dangers that are simultaneously impacting on businesses in the early 21st century:

- Competition for talent and skills in an aging society.

- The pressure for innovation: the necessity to reinvent company value (products and services) in a knowledge-networked global economy.

- Escalating costs: the costs of skilled human resources are growing rapidly, with new approaches required to contain them.

- New work-life-meaning relationships: changing values and lifestyles in society, impacting on attitudes and expectations regarding work and life-meaning in general.

While some of these dangers have been observed for some time already, it is the convergence of the four dangers simultaneously that now provides a critical mass and serves as an impending crisis for most enterprises. And compounding the crisis is the fact that managerial mindsets, attitudes and practices are still largely rooted in 20th century thinking and conditions, which are seriously deficient to handle the challenges. Let's look at each of these dangers in more detail – greater understanding of them is the first step towards the right actions.

Competition for Talent and Skills in an Aging Society

The increasing level of competition for talent and skills is evidenced on country, industry and enterprise levels. On country level, we are witnessing the global shifts in competing demand and supply of workers in health (e.g. nurses, doctors), education (e.g. teachers, professors), R & D (particular types of scientists), human resource professionals, and marketing and sales experts (e.g. global marketing skills). Already, serious conflicts on political levels are arising as top-level talent and skills are being drawn away from other countries (esp. from developing countries, such as many in Africa).

On industry level, we are seeing increasing competition for knowledge workers in e.g. financial services, pharmaceuticals, travel & tourism, information technology (IT), communications, and transport & logistics.

On the enterprise level, we are witnessing the emergence of new practices by forward-thinking companies that are currently experiencing skills shortages: new and creative recruitment practices, targeted retention policies, long-term workforce composition planning, and innovative retirement solutions, by companies such as Dow, IBM, Home Depot, Capital One, Lincoln Financial Services, MITRE Corporation and Novartis. The National Association of Manufacturers in the U.S. warns of a coming 'talent crunch' to be particularly acute in the technical and scientific fields.[7]

How IBM Competes for IT Skills[8]

For some time, IBM has been concerned about the shortage of IT workers and has focused on how to address potential workforce and knowledge needs. The company is working to engage former IBM alumni as an "on demand" via a third-party vendor, bringing retirees back to work on discrete projects. The company also developed a Technical Academic Career Program, which allows workers who are approaching retirement to teach in academia for nearly their same salary. It is also creating additional flexible work options for those employees who are not as close to retirement.

IBM employees work frequently in teams, which creates natural opportunities for sharing knowledge across generations. The company doesn't take this for granted and is developing additional teaming and coaching strategies. For example, the IBM Institute for Knowledge-Based Organizations offers a range of special programs for knowledge transfer, including a day-and-a-half workshop on knowledge sharing, which is also available to IBM customers.

The Pressure for Innovation: The Necessity to Reinvent Company Value (Products & Services) in the Knowledge-Networked Global Economy

Another reason why the aging workforce is becoming a critical issue right now is the global pressures on innovation. It is a well-known fact that since the mid-1990's, the world has shifted from an industrial economy to a knowledge-networked innovation economy – due to advances in communications technology, knowledge-networking, globalization, speed of information exchange, and rates of new product/service innovation combined with increased speed-to-market in globally-integrated demand and supply chains.[9] With a declining and especially aging workforce, the pressure to maintain and expand innovation capacity in enterprises is likely to become severe. Companies will have to find ways to rejuvenate, re-energize and mentally stimulate their aging workforce to achieve this, otherwise they will face loss of competitiveness and sustainability.

Escalating Costs

Companies have been focusing on reduction of costs through downsizing, outsourcing, reengineering and other methods during most of the 1990's and early 2000's. In most instances, admirable cost efficiencies and lean organizations have been successfully achieved. Now, however, the world is entering a new era of unavoidable cost escalations, especially due to the significantly increasing costs of skilled human resources. It is a simple issue of supply and demand: the shrinking supply of talent and skills and the increasing demand for high-level, knowledgeable and innovative labor forces, leading to workforce cost escalations.

Furthermore, the aging workforce requires significant additional investments in the right types of company facilities, health programs, appropriate technological supports, retention and rejuvenation incentives, and further training and development. All of this means an imminent escalation of costs for any enterprise that requires the right types of strategies and operational tools to contain such costs within competitive parameters. It also requires a new mindset concerning employees and their related 'costs': in the future, enterprises will see their workforce increasingly as an 'investment', rather than just costs to be contained or controlled.

New Work-Life-Meaning Relationships

In a knowledge-networked world with changing personal attitudes regarding time, leisure, values and job satisfaction, employees are requiring their talent and skills inputs to have value-added for both organizations and themselves. Work is not any more a means to an end, but also an enriching and fulfilling experience in many different and flexible ways. Unfortunately, concerning their employees most enterprises are still trapped in the traditional work-survival-status-life paradigm of the 20th century. The traditional human resources practices focused on job descriptions, conventional monetary incentives, retirement and succession policies, and traditional recruitment and retention strategies, are not appropriate anymore in the world of an aging (and shrinking) workforce.

A new paradigm, focused on employees' value-added lifestyle with personal meaning, with flexible rewards is emerging, but many companies are bewildered and need strategic and operational guidance. This is a critical challenge today, as it is well known that paradigm shifts occur mainly when the body of contrary evidence (to the traditional paradigm) becomes so large that it causes a sudden and decisive major shift in mindsets.[10] Our contention is that this paradigm shift is now just about occurring, or starting to occur, while the scramble for managerial ways to deal with this is about to happen – and therefore the need for and purpose of this book.

Which Companies and Organizations are Responding to the Challenges?

Some companies and organizations (e.g. NGOs, educational institutions) have been sensing the challenges of the aging workforce, and are responding in various ways. Although still few and far between, these examples serve as powerful indicators of the rising urgency of wisely managing the aging workforce. Some prominent universities have responded to the challenge by recently forming institutes, centers and laboratories to study the aging worker phenomenon and to provide guidance and assistance to company leaders and managers – such as Massachusetts Institute of Technology's Age-Lab, International University of Bremen's Jacobs Center for Lifelong Learning (JCLL), University of St. Gallen's major research focus Work, Aging and Welfare, and various initiatives such as the aging project envisioning a School for Advanced Institutional Leadership (SAIL) at Harvard University.

While several national and supra-national government agencies worldwide have started to focus on the phenomenon of aging populations and their impacts, and sociologists have known about the demographic threat for decades, the evidence from business enterprises is still sparse. Business consulting firms, such as Accenture, Adecco and Roland Berger, have become active with published reports and memoranda, and the incidence of corporate seminars and courses are increasing, especially in Europe. Despite these increasing efforts, what seems to be lacking is an integrated paradigm of managing the aging workforce, the reason for this book.

The following example shows a company in the financial services industry responding to the challenge.

Lincoln Financial Services[11]

Lincoln Financial was concerned enough about its maturing workforce that it launched a taskforce in 2004 to develop a strategic plan to address the issues of recruitment, retention and knowledge transfer. It is also seeking ways to better integrate the mature workers in its workforce.

Traditionally, Lincoln Financial's customer service representatives, as in many companies and industries, are young workers. The company recognized, however, that many customers feel more comfortable discussing financial issues with a mature worker. So it is now finding ways to incorporate mature workers into the customer service workforce.

Lincoln Financial has created a 'paid time off' from the bank, which offers more flexibility than a predetermined allocation of vacation, holiday and sick time. This appeals to mature workers, who may need time off for medical reasons and/or elder care but want to maintain a certain level of privacy.

An example in the non-profit sector is MITRE Corporation, as illustrated below.[12]

The MITRE Corporation

The US headquartered MITRE Corporation is a not-for-profit organization that works in the public interest to provide technical support to the government in systems engineering, research and development, and information technology. It operates federally funded research and development centers (FFRDCs) for the Department of Defense, the Federal Aviation Administration and the Internal Revenue Service. The organization provides technical support to other agencies of the US federal government as well.

The MITRE Corporation is an organization that has always depended upon very experienced mature workers because of the value they bring to its customers and their contributions to the mission of the organization. MITRE's 5,700 scientists, engineers and support specialists – 65 percent of whom have Masters or Ph.D. degrees – are highly valued for their expertise, productivity, creativity and commitment. As of 2003, 71 percent of MITRE employees were 40 years of age or older.

Workers with mature judgment, long-tenure and a unique combination of skills in systems engineering and information technology are essential to the FFRDCs. In addition to their education, knowledge, and experience in these highly technical fields, their loyalty, dedication, and commitment to doing quality work is invaluable. Older workers also compose a large part of MITRE's institutional memory, greatly facilitating knowledge continuity in the knowledge-driven organization.

To ensure the continuation and enrichment of the organizational culture, one of MITRE's diversity committees is looking at generational diversity issues, as well as at knowledge transfer issues. The company provides lots of opportunities for in-house moves, mentoring and training. It offers over 350 courses a year, as well as an "Accelerated Graduate Degree Program," which provides for a paid period off to let individuals focus on studies.

Can the Challenges be Managed? How, What and Where are the Solutions for My Company?

The challenges of an aging workforce can indeed be managed, but as indicated above, it will require a paradigm shift for enterprise leadership and organizational management. Three essential prerequisites of such a paradigm shift are:

- Realization, based on a thorough understanding, of the interrelated challenges concerning the aging workforce (Part I of this book);

- Insight into the implications of an aging workforce of an enterprise's business model (Part II of the book);

- Strategic and operational capabilities to conceive (design) and implement appropriate solutions – what we term 'action fields' in this book – to handle the challenges of an aging workforce (Parts III and IV of the book).

Realization of the Interrelated Challenges of an Aging Workforce

Figure 1.2 illustrates the interrelated challenges of the aging workforce faced by today's enterprises.

The figure demonstrates that the challenges facing enterprises are interrelated and in some instances conflicting. The core challenges are how enterprises, in the context of these pressures, can

a) maintain and even expand their organizational competitive capabilities with appropriate aging workforce actions; and

b) adapt their business models to meet the challenges of new market and customer realities due to an aging society.

Both of these two core challenges are elaborated in the following sections.

Figure 1.2
Interrelated challenges of an aging workforce for enterprises

Insight into the Implications of an Aging Workforce for an Enterprise's Business Model

Every enterprise, be it large or small, or global or local, has a business model, which is simply the particular way it has chosen to do business at a certain point in time.[13] Any business model consists of four basic dimensions: particular market needs served; specific types of product & service propositions ('products'); particular internal and external value chain configurations (designing, producing and delivering the 'products'), with combination of insourced and outsourced functions; and particular competitive policies and capabilities to sustain itself. Any business model is only feasible if it results in sustainable value and rewards to its various stakeholders, including profitability streams for its shareholders. Figure 1.3 illustrates the implications of an aging workforce for an enterprise's business model.

Looking more deeply at the competitive challenges of an aging workforce based on the above enterprise business model implica-

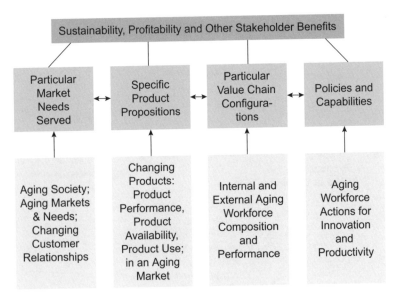

Figure 1.3
Implications of an aging workforce for an enterprise's business model

tions, the major risks can be summarized, and depicted as in Figure 1.4.

Strategic and Operational Capabilities to Devise and Implement Appropriate Solutions in Managing the Challenges of an Aging Workforce

Having a thorough understanding of the challenges of an aging workforce, and having insight into its implications and risks for an enterprise's business model and competitive capabilities, are two elements to enable a paradigm shift for management. A third essential element is to ascertain the 'how to', i.e. how to gain the particular strategic and operational capabilities (e.g. approaches and tools) to deal with the challenges and risks of an aging workforce.

The 5 key capabilities will be outlined in part III of the book:

- Enabling a new *managerial mindset* concerning age, aging and aging workforce facilitation, both internally within the enterprise and with external value-chain partners.

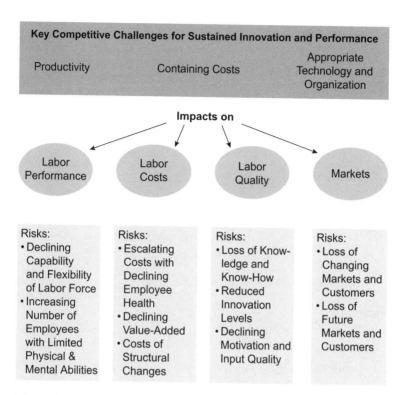

Figure 1.4
Major competitive risks of an aging society and workforce

- How to enable appropriate *knowledge management* processes for an aging workforce: identification, attraction, utilization, dissemination, retention, cooperative sharing, and rejuvenation of relevant knowledge management and further training/development tools.

- Developing *health management* tools for the aging workforce: mental, physical and emotional health management tools, and managing an integrated health management system.

- Designing and facilitating appropriate *working environments and physical tools* for an aging workforce: constructive mobility and active functional reorientation for aging workers, with relevant physical facilities and tools that are age-sensitive.

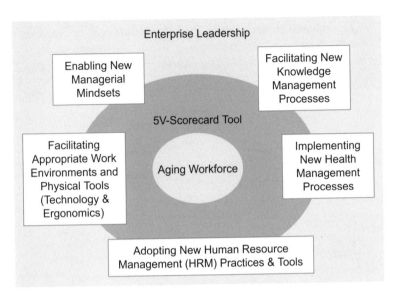

Enterprise Leadership

Enabling New Managerial Mindsets

Facilitating New Knowledge Management Processes

5V-Scorecard Tool

Facilitating Appropriate Work Environments and Physical Tools (Technology & Ergonomics)

Aging Workforce

Implementing New Health Management Processes

Adopting New Human Resource Management (HRM) Practices & Tools

Figure 1.5
The key organizational action fields to manage an aging workforce

- Enabling a redesign of the *human resource management (HRM)* function in the enterprise to incorporate a new focus on the aging workforce, with new HRM tools (e.g. rotation, incentives, rewards) to manage the aging workforce.

Finally, in implementing these five key capabilities an integrated scorecard tool – *the 5V-Scorecard* – to measure the productivity and creativity of the aging workforce of an enterprise, is outlined (Part IV). The nature and operation/use of such a scorecard are highlighted and illustrated.

These 5 key enterprise capabilities, described in organizational action fields, are illustrated in Figure 1.5.

Key Pointers of Chapter 1

- The challenges of an aging workforce for enterprises are large and serious – companies will likely face a critical loss of knowledge and an increasingly severe shortage of skills and labour. A global 'war for talent' is emerging.

- These challenges are critical right now due to proven trends and reputable expectations of shrinking populations, aging workforces, traditional retirement practices, increasing pressures for competitive innovation, escalating costs of human resources, and new work-life-meaning relationships in society.

- Some forward-looking companies are responding to the challenges, such as through alumni-networks, knowledge-sharing workshops, extending retirement age, more flexible working arrangements, etc. There is a need, however, for an integrated approach based on a new paradigm concerning the management of an aging workforce.

- The challenges can be managed, but with three major prerequisites: a thorough understanding of the interrelated challenges; insight into the implications for enterprises' business models; and strategic and operational capabilities concerning a range of 7 key action fields to handle an aging workforce.

2 How Demographic Trends will Impact Economies, Industries and Enterprises

Key Issues of this Chapter

- What is happening to the world's population and workforce?
- What are the nature and impacts of these changes?
- How will economies, industries and enterprises be affected?
- What interventions are possible?
- What should my enterprise be doing?

What is Happening to the World's Population and Workforce?

The world has just passed an important crossover point in human history. For the first time ever, individuals over the age of 55 will represent progressively larger proportions of the global workforce in the industrialized world. Until the Industrial Revolution, population growth was practically the only determinant of economic growth, making up new creative forces and expanding consumer markets. Now, in the early years of the 21st century, economic growth is influenced by a number of global forces, especially the revolution in information communications technologies (ICT), globalization and networking, and the aging of the world's population.

The phenomenon of aging of the industrialized world is driven by three demographic realities[1] and three attitudinal shifts in society. The three demographic realities are: the baby boom generation (born between 1946 and 1964) reaching retirement age; increasing human longevity; and declining birthrates. The three attitudinal shifts in society comprise: the attitude towards work; the attitude towards age; and the attitude towards life in general.

2 Demographic Trends

Demographic Realities

- *The baby boom generation reaching retirement age*

  Nearly one-third of all Americans – 76 million people – were born between 1946 and 1964 (Figure 2.1). That is equivalent to a daily average of over 10,000 births in the United States, with 1,000 in Canada, and similar numbers across Europe and Australia. This fertile period happened between the baby busts of the Depression and World War II, and the Viet Nam era. At such numbers, the boomer generation has repeatedly reshaped especially American and European life and their customs, and fueled health care much of the productivity and innovation of the past several decades. As boomers reach traditional retirement age, the question arises of how corporations will survive the anticipated massive exodus of skills, experience, customer relationships and knowledge – a critical brain drain.

Births in Millions

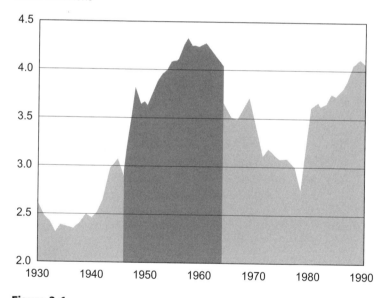

Figure 2.1
The baby boom in the USA: 1946 to 1964
(Source: U.S. Census Bureau)

- *Increasing human longevity*

  Throughout most of human history, the average life expectancy was less than eighteen years. Around 1900, life expectancy at birth in the United States was about forty-seven years; now it is about seventy-seven years (Figure 2.2). A hundred years ago, only 4 percent of the U.S. population was over sixty-five; now it has reached 14 percent and is rising. Thanks to break-throughs in healthcare and other quality-of-life advances, more people are living longer. Consequently, notions of work and life are dramatically shifting. Questions such as the following arise with significant and increasing frequency: What is middle age and old age? When are workers no longer able and productive? At what age do employees stop learning or seeking new challenges, if at all?

Years

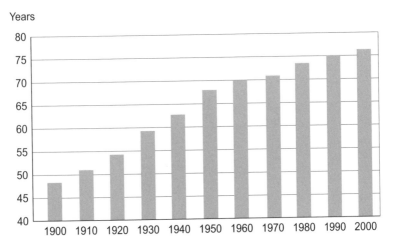

Figure 2.2
Life expectancy at birth in the United States
(Source: U.S. National Center for Health Statistics)

- *Declining birthrates*

  After peaking at 3.7 in the mid-1950s, the average number of children per woman in the United States has declined to 2 by 2000. Nearly 20 percent of baby boomers have no children, and another 25 percent have only one child per family.

2 Demographic Trends

Declining birthrates across industrialized nations are resulting in a recurrent shortage of native-born young workers (Figure 2.3). Countries with birthrates such as Italy's (1.2), Germany's (1.3) and Japan's (1.4) are well below the replacement rate of 2.1 children per woman, with a resulting shrinking of their population and workforce – now becoming the focus of major concern to their governments and business enterprises.

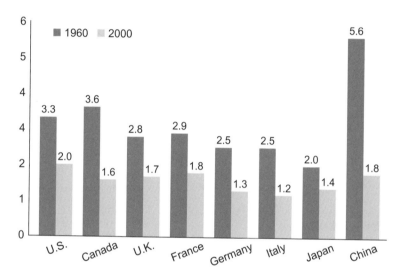

Figure 2.3
Total fertility rate in selected countries: 1960 and 2000
(Source: United Nations Population Division)

These three demographic realities drive the so-called age wave, an unprecedented shift in the age distribution of the population. How global is this wave? Figure 2.4 depicts the projected growth or shrinkage of the working-age populations of eight countries. The United States appears to experience modest but steady growth, whereas the United Kingdom, after a grow-then-shrink cycle, will have the same number of workers in 2050 as in 2000. China follows a similar up-and-down pattern, ending with 5 percent more working-age people in 2050 than 2000 – but that means 45 million more people. Unless birthrates or immigration rates change radically, the compounded effects of the declines depicted in Figure 2.4 will reduce the German workforce by 25 percent in 2050, the Italian by 30 percent, and the Japanese by 38 percent. Throughout most of Europe, including the former Eastern Bloc countries, the pattern is the same.

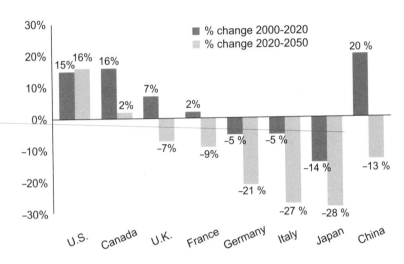

Figure 2.4
Percent change in working-age population: 20 to 64 years
(Source: U.S. Census Bureau International Data Base)

Attitudinal Shifts in Society

- *The attitude towards work*

    Work, in terms of personal investment of talent and skills, is increasingly seen as open-ended, creative, value-adding, and sharing with others, in contrast to the Newtonian-based attitudes of the past three centuries – of work being rigidly prescribed, constraining and toil-sweat based. The knowledge-networked 21st century recognizes that work (value-added) now is largely viewed as being centered on knowledge and innovation, with even menial jobs offering creative opportunities.

- *The attitude towards age*

    The concept of age is ever shifting further in chronological terms – in 1950 a person aged 60 was considered 'old', while in

2 Demographic Trends

2005 this has shifted to age 70 and even older. Increasing examples of active corporate leaders, political leaders, respected educationists and top-level scientists aged 70 and beyond are known, with the management guru Peter Drucker publishing leading managerial thought articles well into his 90s.

- *The attitude towards life in general*

  The value and meaning of life is shifting fast in society: With greater prosperity and ability to cater to life's basic needs in most parts of the world, people increasingly see work as adding value to their lives, and making a meaningful difference in society – work to live, rather than live to work.

These forces, both demographic and attitudinal, are shaping today's workforce. Their impacts are outlined in the next sections.

The Nature and Impacts of an Aging Workforce

The 21st century workforce will be significantly different than the workforce of the past century. Their nature will be:[2]

- *Relatively much older chronologically*

  After a steady decline in the proportion of older workers through the 1990s, the percentage is now on the rise. The proportion of over-55 workers in the U.S. declined from 18% in 1970 to 11% in 2000. By 2015, this group will have significantly increased to represent 20%. Driven by ever-longer life spans and lower birth rates, older workers will continue to grow as a portion of the available labor pool throughout the century. Enterprises cannot afford not to leverage this talent – businesses will need both the numbers and, more importantly, the skills represented in this growing cohort. *And, as research by the Concours Group shows, most mature employees are more satisfied and engaged, happier on the job and better adjusted to the workplace than younger workers on average.*[3]

- *Limited in availability and lacking key skills*

  The workforce is set to grow slowly or decline in size in most developed countries. In the U.S., the workforce is forecast to grow by only a fraction of a percentage point a year for most of the first half of the century. The total working age population will grow at 2 to 3% per decade from now through 2030 and then increase to 3 to 4% per decade through 2050 – still only a fraction of a percent per year. By comparison, the rates have been 12 to 15% per decade for most of the second half of the 20th century. Industrial growth will be constrained by the availability of labor if we continue to operate in an old mindset, even taking labor-replacing technologies into account.

The workforce is expected to be deficient in the optimum mix of talent needed by industries. There will be shortages of many key skill sets, and excesses of other less-strategic capabilities. Many high skill areas, such as engineering disciplines, are already approaching critical shortages. For example, the average age of petroleum engineers in the U.S. is approaching 54, while many of the oil companies still have lucrative early retirement programs that will allow these scarce resources to leave the workforce at 55.

The world seems to be on the brink of critical shortages in a number of key skill areas, assuming aging workforce and retirement approaches remain unchanged.

- *Physically dispersed*

  Work will increasingly be done anywhere, anytime, rather than in fixed locations and on schedules of 9 am to 5 pm. *Managing the workforce will become more and more analogous to the challenge of managing customers* – developing relationships, loyalty and maintaining active connections will be key issues.

- *Inventing new life and work stages*

  As a result of increasing health and longevity, most individuals will experience a new life stage – a prolonged period of time after primary parenting duties are fulfilled but before they will look, feel, or act "old." *This 20 to 30 year period,* unprecedented in history, *will offer exciting opportunities for continued creativity, innovation and productive working life contributions.*

- *Highly diverse values and work assumptions*

  The workforce is increasingly populated by individuals with widely differing values and assumptions about work itself.

These divergent attitudes toward work will be one of the most important forms of workplace diversity during this century, challenging employers to find innovative ways to understand and respond to disparate needs. Many employees today are searching for "additional returns" than they are normally able to draw from their work experience. The point of mid-life today is often a reflection of the perception of the impact of one's life on the world. As employees reach whatever milestone triggers a sense of middle age, they are increasingly reprioritizing to live up to the idealistic values formed in their youth. In greater numbers today, employees are asking whether the paths they have taken are indeed consistent with the values they formed earlier in life. *Coupled with a general disillusionment with large corporate life, many workers are emotionally pulling away – detaching from "work", and depriving businesses of essentially needed energy, innovation, and drive.*

These elements of the nature of a fast-changing workforce represent a major challenge for all types of organizations. *While the characteristics of the workforce are changing, the question arises if significant advances in technology will compensate for the aging and declining pool of skilled workers. The simple answer is no, because technological advances will both reinforce (i.e. exacerbate) the aging workforce challenges, and also allow individual workers more options for other types of economic and societal activities.* The significant advances in technology driving the way businesses operate are:[4]

- *Instant and cheap coordination*

  Technologies such as service-oriented web architecture, radio frequency identification chips and sensor nodes will provide extraordinary opportunities for coordination and collaboration. Very soon, smart objects, intelligent sensors and ubiquitous connectivity will be everywhere, on everything, and "always active." Instead of processing data and information, businesses will be based on processing knowledge about events in real time. In place of waiting for operator input, sensor networks will respond directly to their environment.

- *More efficient markets*

  The pressure on enterprises for increased levels of productivity will be unrelenting and undiminishing. The easy availability of inexpensive coordination technology will make the relationship between businesses, suppliers, consumers and other stakeholders much more efficient. More efficient markets will threaten any firm whose business model embraces inefficiencies. Consumers will find it easy to collect information, compare prices, and select multiple providers based on the core competencies of each provider, and will be able to improve their negotiation for the best deals possible.

- *Participative decision-making*

  Technology will allow organizations to conduct their governance processes in fundamentally different ways – ways that are more compatible with the values and preferences of this century's aging workforce. Over the next several decades, the trend for hierarchy to increasingly give way to lateral communication among relatively autonomous, entrepreneurial groups and 'communities of practice', will continue apace. As it becomes both economically and logistically feasible to obtain input from a large number of people, opinion polling and even virtual democratic elections will come into the workplace. Market-based mechanisms allowing workers to offer and make their own mutual agreements, as contractors and freelancers around specific projects, will be commonplace in the near future.

- *Networks of small, highly focused firms*

  Networked technology facilitates the unbundling of integrated corporations, leading to more focused companies and denser linkages of value chains. Smaller firms, specializing around core competencies, will proliferate in the 21st century. Coordination-intense, networked organizational structures enabled by mobile communications technology, will allow firms to adjust continuously to changing requirements for different combinations of skills and resources.

- *Strategies based on agile initiatives*

  Top-down direction and annual strategic planning cycles are already being replaced by rapid waves of short-term experimental initiatives, brought into focus and cohered by a shared view of a company's long-term strategic direction. Growth will emerge from the creativity and innovation that comes from a shift in control: top-down to bottom-up in flatter hierarchies – driven by engaged employees, partners, network agencies, and even customers.

The need to create a highly engaged network of diverse talent will become critically important to meeting the agile operating styles required for the 21st century enterprise. The impacts of these changes in the global workforce and of the technologies that enable work are likely to be profound:

- *The demise of "retirement"*

  Retirement is a relatively modern social concept, and our parents were the first guinea pigs and practitioners. For almost all of history, until the early 1900s, people worked until they died. Today, the average worker in developed countries retires at 62 – and, with rising life expectancies, can thereafter expect twenty or more years of active life. *Over this century, we will increasingly discard the concept of "retirement" as we know it today – to be replaced by a more flexible view of work that is intermingled with periods of leisure, personal development, and community enrichment throughout all of individual lifespans.* Already, as much as 34% of all U.S. workers say they never plan to retire.

- *New career path structures*

  Rather than the cliff-shaped career paths of the past century – individuals on an ever-upward path toward ever-greater "success" – 21st century careers will be bell-shaped. *A career deceleration phase in one's 50s through 80s will parallel the career development phase of one's 20s through 40s.* After achieving peak levels of responsibility in one's mid-career, individuals will be able to continue to contribute to businesses in legitimate, respected, although less intense ways.

- *Multiple hiring options*

  Individuals will enter into new careers at multiple points throughout their lives. *Older workers will accept "entry" level jobs, as ways into new lines of work or flexible options suited to a preferred lifestyle.*

- *Flexible and project-oriented work arrangements*

  In an aging society, more flexible work arrangements are both necessary and possible. Corporations will provide personal variability around how individuals are compensated, managed, and matched with different types of tasks. Project-based work will become the norm – many workers will operate as "intellectual free-lancers" assembled by project over the Web, as needed. *Already, nearly 50% of workers who plan to work during traditional retirement years say that they would prefer cyclical arrangements – periods of full-time work interspersed with periods of no work – over more conventional part-time types of work.*

- *Small firm employment*

  Those employees who do affiliate with a single enterprise will be increasingly likely to be employed by small firms. Small firms will become more prevalent over the century based on changes in technology. Today, small firms on average have two-and-a-half times more highly engaged workers than do large corporations (32% versus 13%). *Although large firm employers generally offer more benefits, they get less engagement in return than smaller firm employers.*

- *Home-based and virtual work*

  Workers will increasingly work from home or other flexible locations as technology continues to enable remote and mobile work, and workers who are accustomed to interacting through technology become a dominant presence in the workforce. Today, almost three-quarters of the workforce still work at a fixed location. However, this percentage will decline over the century as a confluence of technology enablement, employee preference, and corporate cost pressures drive organizations to seek ways to shift away from "bricks and mortar" and associated overhead.

- *Ownership of technology*

  Young workers entering the workforce today "own" their own technology – it is as much a part of their personal being as wallets are to their parents. Soon, the concept of corporations supplying computers or mobile phones will be as outdated as the clothing allowances of the 1950s or company calculators of the 1970s. All tomorrow's employees will ask is that business "beams them in." *Security will be replaced by selection as a core concern, since hiring ethical individuals will be more effective than trying to control access in an increasingly ubiquitous world.*

- *Job sharing for balanced lives*

  For various reasons, today's worker cohorts are less willing to devote all of their life's energies to "work". Baby boomers want to devote a part of their activities to idealistic goals. *Younger cohorts have* an inherent reluctance for large institutional affiliation, and *a tendency to prefer independent and smaller-networked relationships.* Workers in this century will be increasingly articulate in demanding work relationships with corporations that allow them to retain a greater degree of control and flexibility required to pursue other activities equally successfully.

- *Significantly changed patterns of personal learning and health management*

  The manner in which today's younger workers have learned to learn is radically different from their predecessors. *Rather than linear learning from authoritative sources, younger workers tend to learn through a process of assembly* – putting pieces of knowledge and information from a variety of sources together. This experimental and action learning approach, coupled with technology's increasing network-interactions and information search capabilities – will increasingly spill over into the way work gets done.

- *Healthcare benefits*

  Health will be an immensely important issue and continuing focus for decisions in the home, workplace and community. Healthcare benefits is likely to be the single unifying desire of the 21st century workforce. Among more detailed elements of the deal, *health care coverage is already workers' top priority by far.*

The above-mentioned impacts of changes in the global workforce, especially in developed countries, are not entirely unknown, new or totally unanticipated. However, history has shown that most enterprises adapt to major shifts in markets, capabilities, workforce or competition only when they are forced to do so. *Those enterprises that survive and sustain themselves are those that have a proactive disposition and not only realize the trends and impacts of an aging workforce, but also how they are likely to be affected and how to respond wisely to the challenges.*

How will Economies, Industries and Enterprises be Affected?

Most economies, industries and enterprises as we know them today are not aligned with the needs and values of the 21st century aging workforce. Those that are responding, such as some governments increasing the age of retirement of workers from 60 to 65, and even 67 (in the U.K.), do it in a partial or piece-meal fashion. Few large organizations are really preparing for the transformation of the workforce: In its 2003 "Older Worker Survey" in the U.S, the Society for Human Resource Management (SHRM) reports that one-third of HR professionals say their companies are doing nothing to prepare for demographic change in the workforce.[5] Those who say they are preparing are focused on training and succession planning. Only 7 percent have plans to deal with an anticipated retirement wave.

Labor shortages affect different economies, industries and employers in different ways. Where many public utilities face a mass retirement of skilled technicians well before 2010, the medical profession has needed nurses for many years. Already, some developed economies, such as in Europe, the USA and Japan are competing for skilled professionals and drawing them especially from developing countries where reward packages are relatively low. A widely reported estimate in the U.S. is a skilled worker shortfall of 10 million by 2010.[6] *The Employment Policy Foundation (EPF) estimates that 80% of the impending global labor shortage will involve skills, not numbers of workers potentially available.*[7]

A complex set of variables shapes the nature, timing and extent of these impacts:[8]

- *Economic conditions and the rate of job creation* govern the demand for workers. Job creation has been accelerating in the U.S., and the 23 million net new jobs this decade, as estimated by the EPF, will outstrip the supply of new workers by a wide margin.[9]

- *Productivity gains* reduce the demand for labor. Improved automation and information flow enables companies to do more with fewer employees, and so economists no longer peg economic growth to labor force growth as they did when the economy centered on manufacturing and manual labor. Today's information-based work lends itself to more extensive automation and potentially higher rates of productivity growth. Thus, a sustained rate of 2 percent productivity growth would reduce any labor shortage by two-thirds, but there are likely ceilings to productivity increases in some industries.

- *The net export of jobs* reduces labor shortages. The number of jobs currently offshored in an average year amounts to only two-tenths of 1 percent of total jobs in the U.S. High-end estimates peg about 2 million jobs moving offshore in the U.S. in the first decade of the 21st century – a significant number, but not regarded as enough to offset anticipated skills and labor shortages. Labor markets, like consumer and capital markets, continue to globalize. More of today's information-based work can be performed anywhere in the world.

- *Immigration policies*, including the number of work visas allowed for skilled workers, will affect the labor pool. By 2020, immigration is expected to account for virtually all of the United States' net workforce growth. North America is in a better situation than some European and Asian nations where immigration is tightly controlled and birthrates fall far below replacement levels. By 2020, the overall European Union (EU) economy will need either a two-thirds increase in productivity or a significant enlargement of the labor force via immigration to avoid contraction; Germany alone is likely to need a million working-age immigrants per year to maintain its workforce.[10] EU members face a major dilemma in deciding whether to embrace proposed EU rules on the free flow of labor, or to protect local jobs.

- *Education* – not just the number of workers but what they can actually do, factors heavily in almost every new job created. The technological demands of even "unskilled" entry-level jobs are increasing, and professional and technical fields are already experiencing labor shortages. The BLS estimates that 56 percent of workers gather, process, or use some form of automated information in their work. According to the EPF, 35 percent of the labor force is active in management, professional, and technical occupations that demand extensive education, ongoing training, independent thinking, and decisive action.

The BLS estimates that one in five new jobs this decade will be in business services, the fastest-growing sector. Other 'hot' occupations include various categories of computer engineers and users (e.g., desktop publishing), nurses, medical and home care assistants, sales and customer service representatives, general office clerks, food preparers and servers, and security guards. It is expected that by 2010, 25 percent of all American workers will be in professional occupations, the most information-intensive of all. Overall, the United States will need 18 million new college degree holders by 2012 to cover job growth and replace retirees but, at current graduation rates, will be 6 million short.[11]

- *Workforce participation rates* will affect the labor pool. Obviously, if more people choose to work, then the talent deficit narrows. However, the overall participation rate of about 67 percent is holding steady. The rate among men, currently about 75 percent, is declining slightly; the rate among women of over 60 percent continues rising slowly, and every percentage point increase means another million workers. But compared to the increases of recent decades (the rate doubled between 1950 and 2000), women's participation has essentially leveled off. There remains considerable room for growth among older workers: those in the fifty-five to sixty-four age range participate at a 60 percent rate, those over sixty-five at a 13 percent rate, and both numbers are trending upward. The EPF notes that there are 13.6 million college degree holders not in the workforce – predominantly retirees over age sixty.[12] As we strongly argue in this book, to minimize the pending labor and skills shortage, managers must adopt new, mutually beneficial ways to retain and re-activate older workers.

2 Demographic Trends

In summary, there will be too few young workforce entrants to replace the labor, skills and talents of the coming wave of retirees. The question is: How critical is the situation? The Employment Policy Foundation projects a shortage of several million U.S. workers this decade, 10 million by 2015, and 35 million by 2030.[13] The EPF approach makes the most sense to us because it compares the projected labor force available against that needed to produce enough goods and services to maintain the historic growth trend in per capita consumption. The current U.S. annual gross domestic product is about $12 trillion. Given that the average worker produces about $78,000 worth of goods and services (in today's dollars), a shortfall of 10 million workers means an economy almost $3 trillion smaller. In other words, a large and prolonged worker shortage could severely reduce the current standard of living. More detailed than Figure 1.1, Figure 2.5 depicts the critical situation now emerging.

In Figure 2.5, note that the lines representing labor needed and available are starting to diverge from 2006 onwards. Note also

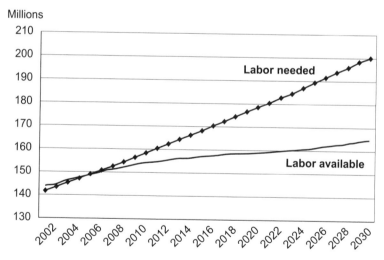

Figure 2.5
Projected workforce shortages 2007-2030
(Source: Employment Policy Foundation analysis and projections of U.S. Census, Bureau of Labor Statistics, and Bureau of Economics Analysis data)

that the bigger problem is not the number of available workers but the availability of skills to fill today's and tomorrow's jobs.

Wider Political and Societal Implications[14]

The wider political and societal implications of the aging of the baby boom generation, increasing longevity, and declining birthrates are enormous. Politically, most developed countries are becoming gerontocracies. Today's senior citizens have the lowest poverty level, are the richest segment of society, and wield unrivaled and ever-increasing political clout. People typically vote in proportion to their age (less than one-third of twenty-year-olds vote, while over 70 percent of seventy-year-olds do), and so politicians have learned to cater to the senior vote.

Figure 2.6 illustrates how population aging is expected by the OECD to place a growing economic burden on workers.[15]

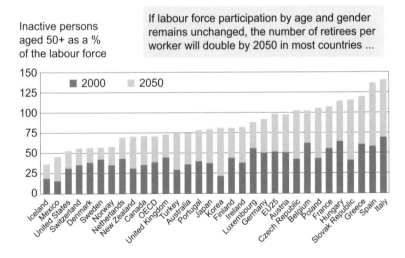

Figure 2.6
Population aging and the expected growing burden on workers
(Source: OECD)

Some countries face much bigger challenges and adjustments than others, according to the OECD, as illustrated in Table 2.1.[16]

2 Demographic Trends

Table 2.1

The size of the challenge for various OECD countries (Source: OECD)

Participation rate of 50 to 64 year olds, 2004	Projected change in the old-age dependency ratio, 2000 to 2050		
	Moderate	*Large*	*Very large*
High	Denmark, Iceland, Norway, Sweden, Switzerland, United States	Canada, New Zealand	Japan
Average	Netherlands, United Kingdom	Australia, Finland, France, Germany, Mexico, Ireland	Czech Republic, Korea, Portugal
Low	Belgium, Luxembourg, Turkey	Austria, Hungary	Greece, Italy, Poland, Slovak Republic, Spain

The key issue that arises is:

- *How should companies and governments plan for the shrinking number of young workers, young taxpayers, and young consumers?*

Most marketing is still youth oriented (or "youth obsessed") even though today's mature adults (those over fifty) control two-thirds of the accumulated wealth in developed countries. Baby boomers will be the most financially powerful generation of mature consumers ever.

Key questions being posed are:

- *What happens to marketing and product development when 80 percent of the consumer growth comes from the fifty-plus age group?*

- *How will businesses maintain brand loyalty when customers reinvent themselves at forty, sixty, and eighty years old?*

- *Will boomers, who have been active spenders in their middle years, become more frugal as they mature?*

- *What happens to families as people provide more care to their parents than to their children?*

Thirty percent of the workforce is already pressurized between obligations to children and aging parents. In the coming decades, four-generation families will become the norm.

- *How will couples reinvent their marriages repeatedly because of the length of life?*

Furthermore:

- *What will be new sources of economic and productivity growth as workforce growth slows?*

- *Will equity markets be driven by higher savings rates or by flagging consumer markets?*

- *How can countries continue to support generous pension programmes when the ratio of workers to retirees continues to diminish?*

Already, General Motors and other long-established corporations have far more retirees than active workers. In the United States, there is more retired military staff than there are individuals in military service.

- *Can developing countries with relatively young population distributions develop the business and educational infrastructure to capitalize on the situation?*

These questions obviously deserve acute attention from governments, social organizations, market researchers and business enterprises. The focus of this book is on managing the aging workforce to assist business enterprises, but obviously they will also have an important role in public and social policies that affect these business challenges.

What Interventions are Possible?

The significant challenges and their impacts, especially for the aging workforce and enterprise management, require urgent and immediate interventions. Some actions will have only medium to long-term impacts, but many offer solutions in the short term. Furthermore, the challenges should not be viewed only as problems, but also as opportunities to achieve sustainable and growing competitive advantages for particular enterprises.

Enterprises must now start putting the same energy into optimizing the relationships with and within the workforce as they have invested in optimizing processes and technologies in the 20th century. Certainly, companies must continue to employ technology to its fullest potential, ensuring that every member of the corporation, from the Board of Directors to entry-level employees, has the skill to employ technology comfortably and appropriately. But this century will be about something fundamentally different: Rather than standardizing work-to-work relationships, the 21st century will both require and allow greater variation.

Aligning all the elements of the employee experience – everything that touches or influences the workforce, including the style of management, the nature of the job, forms of compensation, work environment, and even the fundamental approaches and philosophies of the firm's leadership team – with each other and with the preferences of targeted employees, will be the essence of creating a highly engaged, innovative and productive workforce.

In some countries, governments are now looking seriously at abolishing mandatory retirement ages (e.g. the U.K.), while in Asia the government of Singapore is considering the extension of the retirement age. Some Japanese employers are offering short-term contracts to former employees, enabling them to meet specific needs without assuming the burden of long-term commitment to new employees. The Internal Revenue Service in the U.S.A. is proposing regulations for voluntary phased retirements.

Switzerland's legislation enables people who stay at work for up to five years beyond the statutory retirement age to increase their state pension by up to SFr 5,000 (about $ 3,800) a year when they eventually draw it. That helps explain why more than 60% of all 55- to 64-year-old Swiss are in work, compared to less than 30% in Italy and Belgium. For Italy, which has one of the lowest fertility rates in Europe and one of the lowest average retirement ages, the demographic cliff is a precipice looming very threateningly in its society.

In some countries the tax system works against older workers. Britain will not let a taxpayer receive a pension and a salary from the same employer. In America, pension schemes will often withhold benefits from a retired person if he/she is rehired or works for more than 40 hours a month. Companies wishing to hire their pensioners have to find ways around the rules. Japanese companies such as Mazda, for example, rehire retirees on one-year renewable contracts.

Over the past several years, the focus in the EU has changed from preventing age discrimination to mobilizing the aging workforce.[17] In recent summits, EU leaders have set two goals to encourage member countries to focus on this aging workforce problem. At the 2001 European Council, EU members agreed on a goal of achieving a 50 percent employment rate for older workers (55 to 64 years).[18] In 2002, the Barcelona European Council identified the retirement age of older workers as a common European problem and concluded that the exit ages of older workers for each country in the EU should be raised by five years by 2010.[19] A recent report by the Commission of the European Communities indicated that while some advances have been made in reaching these targets, overall, the EU is "still far short of both targets, and much stronger efforts are needed to make the necessary progress towards both targets."[20]

Figure 2.7 summarizes the current status of the 25 European Union countries with respect to their progress toward the Stockholm and Barcelona targets, as of 2002.

On an enterprise level, some researchers and observers have been offering suggestions for various types of interventions, and also examples of companies using different forms of interventions. Some are highlighted here and more extensively discussed in the subsequent chapters.

Jaworski offers the following recommendations:[21]

- Provide flexible work arrangements or telework opportunities to assist those with care-giving responsibilities and those who need to keep post-retirement responsibilities.

- Create career development and training opportunities for mature workers.

- Provide opportunities for mature workers to become mentors in the workplace to facilitate the transfer of knowledge and skills.

2 Demographic Trends

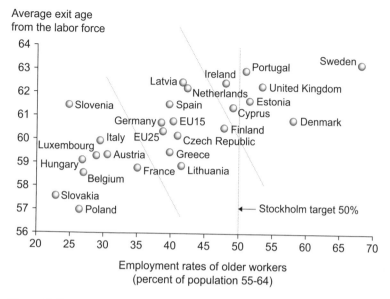

Average exit age
from the labor force

Figure 2.7
Status of EU countries regarding progress toward targets for aging workers
(Source: Commission of the European Communities)

- Offer work-life services that help older workers to proactively manage concerns via one-stop access to information and consultation.

- Develop a retiree relations program to create a pool of trained and motivated workers.

- Encourage a corporate culture that demonstrably values older workers. This could include offering training on older-worker issues for younger supervisors and managers.

Foster suggests actions to both identify organizational needs (e.g. identification of knowledge issues) and to aid knowledge retention.[22] The latter includes managing and training of talent, alignment with customer needs (e.g. building a mature workforce around core client/customer needs), building a retiree network, and broadening succession planning.

De Long identifies four areas requiring management's attention:[23]

- Developing processes and systems to capture and share the critical knowledge by those who are eligible for retirement.

- Exploring new outsourcing models for core tasks.

- Ensuring that the enterprise's culture is aligned to support the future required workforce.

- Reinventing recruitment processes.

Dychtwald, Erickson and Morison suggest three major areas of how companies can retain the skills of employees well past the traditional age of retirement – whereby employees can become lifelong contributors:[24]

- Creating a culture that honors experience.

- Offering flexible work arrangements.

- Introducing flexible retirement.

IBM Business Consulting Services recommend that companies consider six strategies:[25]

- Redirect recruiting and sourcing efforts to include mature workers.

- Retain valued employees through developing alternative work arrangements.

- Preserve critical knowledge before it walks out the door.

- Provide opportunities for workers to continually update their skills.

- Facilitate the coexistence of multiple generations in the workforce.

- Help ensure that mature workers are able to use technology effectively in the workplace.

Some companies have begun to adapt their workplaces to older workers. *Deere & Company*, an industrial equipment manufacturer based in Illinois, USA, has 46,000 employees of which about 35% are over 50 and a number are in their 70s. Its policy is to recruit people who will stay with the company for the rest of their careers. The tools it uses to achieve that – flexible working, telecommuting, and so forth – also coincidentally help older workers to extend their working lives. The company spends considerable effort on the ergonomics of its factories, making jobs there less tiring, which enables older workers to stay at them for longer.[26]

Likewise, for more than a decade, *Toyota*, arguably the world's most advanced automobile manufacturer, has adapted its workstations to older workers. The shortage of skilled labor available to the automotive industry (especially engineers) again has made it unusually keen to recruit older workers. *BMW* recently set up a factory in Leipzig, Germany, that expressly sets out to employ people over the age of 45. Other firms are polishing their alumni networks. *IBM* uses its network to recruit retired people for particular projects. *Ernst & Young*, a professional-services firm, has about 30,000 registered alumni, and about 25% of its "experienced" new recruits are "boomerangs" (former employees who return after an absence).

Monsanto Co., a multinational company based in Missouri, USA, brings back retirees as temporary workers or part-timers to fill gaps and reduce costs.[27] Monsanto's Retiree Resource Corps has more than 800 participating retirees who can work up to 999 hours per year – less than half the usual time. Monsanto estimates that it saves 12 to 15 percent by using retirees instead of traditional 'temps'. The program also helps Monsanto transfer both corporate culture and technical knowledge to younger employees.

Home Depot, the hardware store chain, hires many employees over the age of 50 because of their skills, work ethic, motivation and maturity. This strategy has proven tremendously successful. Home Depot is experiencing the benefits that older workers bring to the workplace, and continues to proactively recruit older employees.

Avis Rent-a-Car noticed that its retired part-time car shuttlers received fewer tickets for traffic violations and were much less likely to scrape, scratch, or bang up its rental cars. Avis began actively recruiting retired people by using some rather unorthodox and imaginative techniques, including handing out information about employment opportunities in the early mornings at shopping malls. The result was an increase in the number of older employees hired and a corresponding decrease in expenses as traffic violations and accident rates decreased significantly.

What Should My Enterprise Be Doing?

The various suggestions and recommendations offered by observers and researchers listed above, as well as the emerging corporate initiatives indicated in the previous section, are valuable but can be confusing due to their varied nature and often overlapping points. It is important that an integrated approach is adopted, with both strategic and operational tools that are simple and practical to use and measure.

First of all, it is important that an enterprise adopts the right mindset, based on a sound understanding of the implications of an aging workforce for its business model, and with integrated objectives concerning each element of its business model as well as for each of its critical managerial areas – including human resources management, work environment management, knowledge management, health management, and functional management areas. Figure 1.3 in Chapter 1 illustrates a typical enterprise business model and its various elements, with critical management areas to be integrated for managing an aging workforce.

Secondly, the key managerial capabilities to manage the aging workforce must be understood, as well as the particular approaches and tools to enable these to be installed – these concern knowledge management capabilities, health management tools, appropriate working environment and physical tools, a geared human resources management function, and productivity and creativity measuring capabilities, all focused on the aging workforce.

Finally, the leadership requirements to guide and enable appropriate management of the aging workforce need to be understood and embedded in the enterprise.

These areas of action, as depicted in Figure 1.5 in Chapter 1, are outlined and discussed in the rest of the book.

Key Pointers of Chapter 2

- The phenomenon of aging of the industrialized world is driven by three demographic realities and three attitudinal shifts in society: demographic realities of a boom in people now starting to retire, increasing longevity, and declining birthrates; while attitudinal shifts towards work, age and life in general is impacting severely on the nature, availability and capabilities of the workforce.

- The impacts of these realities and shifts include the end of "retirement" as we know it, new career paths, flexible work arrangements, different paths of personal learning, health as a core value, and customized employment. For enterprises it is especially critical to retain its "store" of knowledge, and expand its creativeness and productivity for sustained competitiveness.

- Different economies, industries and enterprises will be differently affected by the aging workforce. It is estimated that 80 % of the impending global labor shortage will involve skills, and not numbers of workers potentially available. The competition for skilled labor between countries, regions, industries and enterprises is already becoming evident, and will increase significantly in the future.

- Various types of interventions to meet the challenges and likely impacts of an aging workforce are being suggested or recommended by various observers, and examples of actions by forward-looking firms are emerging. However, these are still mainly partial, piece-meal and confusing, with the need for a new integrated managerial paradigm and toolbox.

- Enterprises should adopt an integrated approach to manage the aging workforce, based on the right mindset – understanding its business model in relation to the aging workforce – and integrated objectives, holistic management of key managerial capabilities, and the right leadership approach.

PART II

Managerial Objectives

3 Company Objectives to Increase the Value (V) of the Aging Workforce for an Enterprise

Key Issues of this Chapter

- The necessity of clear, integrated objectives to increase the value of an aging workforce
- Who is responsible for setting these objectives?
- The particular types of objectives necessary
- Objectives in each of the five key organizational action fields
- Towards integrated aging-focused workforce objectives

The Necessity of Clear, Integrated Objectives to Increase the Value of an Aging Workforce

As the significant forces of changing workforce demographics, changing customer compositions, and changing technologies gather in strength and momentum, enterprises have to be clear about their overall enterprise objectives to sustain and increase the value of an aging workforce. Furthermore, there have to be technical objectives – in terms of enterprise performance and business growth – as well as human objectives in terms of employees' mental, physical and emotional health in surviving organizational and societal upheavals. In an overall context, the necessity for such objectives becomes clear when viewing several key dimensions and facing crucial questions:[1]

- *Productivity*

  What would happen to an organization's productivity if it cannot obtain the workers needed, or if there is a large turnover in its young workers?

What if many of its best workers leave via retirement or dissatisfaction with their overall work situation?

Particular objectives to maintain and increase productivity of an aging workforce are essential.

- *Innovation and business growth*

  What happens if innovative capabilities, creative and energetic sparks, and business growth initiatives start declining?

  Objectives to sustain levels of innovative energies and business growth dynamics with an inevitably aging workforce are crucial to increase enterprise performance.

- *Work processes*

  How does an organization organize a mix and range of diverse employees to collaborate productively?

  How does it capitalize on their diversity?

  What happens when employees' work-style differences – including productive team structures, preferred training methods, proficiency with technology, and attitudes toward authority – become more pronounced?

  With such diverse work arrangements as job sharing, telecommuting, and flexitime, how can the workplace remain cohesive, communicative, and productive?

- *Learning capabilities*

  What happens to institutional knowledge when those who truly understand the business, the customers, and the organization retire all at once?

  How can employers satisfy the thirst for deeper knowledge and continuous learning among the best and brightest employees?

  Does the organization really know how to reengage, retrain, and reignite a fifty- or sixty-year-old?

  Does it know how to accommodate the various learning styles of different age cohorts?

- *Leadership and management*

  What happens when retirement depletes the executive ranks?

What kind of talent will the organization need to lead a thoroughly ethnic-, gender-, lifestyle-, and age-diverse workforce?

Can human resource managers model these skills and develop training programs? How about everyday management?

How does one manage diverse and multigenerational groups effectively?

What managerial or leadership style will bridge different generational expectations?

- *Identity, culture and continuity*

  How will the organization maintain its culture and identity with an increasingly diverse workforce, increasing worker mobility and turnover, and more geographically dispersed work groups?

  How will corporate mergers, divestitures, and other reorganizations factor in aging workforces?

  What will hold an organization together if it outsources or offshores more work?

  How will the brain drain of retirement and other departures affect its institutional memory?

- *Global competitiveness*

  How does an organization remain globally competitive if its workforce demographics are strategically disadvantageous?

  How should it compete for top talent in increasingly global labor markets?

  How can it respond quickly and flexibly and serve global customers coherently, given the many forces fragmenting its workforce?

In view of these key dimensions and crucial questions concerning an enterprise's continued sustainability, all elements of an enterprise's business model and performance should be reviewed to devise particular objectives concerning the dramatic onset of an aging workforce.

Who is Responsible for Setting These Objectives?

The responsibility for setting workforce objectives are primarily with two people: the Chief Executive Officer (CEO) and the head of human resources (HR).[2] As the major enabling driving force of an enterprise, and the person responsible for its overall performance and sustainability, the CEO sets the organization's direction and goals, and ensures that the organization has the dynamic business model, processes and assets – including capital, facilities, technology, and people – to meet those goals. Depending on business conditions, the CEO may focus on different capabilities and resources – for example, securing cash flow and capital in recessions, or updating technology and production facilities during expansions.

The company General Electric is renowned for its investment in developing the performance and potential of the top levels of management – and requiring that these managers do the same in their parts of the business. For GE, the result is a continuous and coordinated attention to talent, and the assignments and challenges that will stretch workers' capabilities. Importantly, besides leadership development and succession, CEOs today should monitor the changing demographic composition of their workforces and recruiting pools. They should understand the overall requirements, flow and bottlenecks of talent throughout their organizations. Most fundamentally, CEOs should insist on a visionary, coherent workforce goal and objectives that maintain the talent supply during significant workforce changes and shortages.

To purposefully initiate the development of those objectives and strategies, the CEO and executive team must own these challenges visibly and collectively, because many of the tactics that will serve and appeal to present and future employees will require significant deviation from past practices and established attitudes. Programs involving flexible work arrangements, for example, often require the genuine goal commitment and explicit objectives-setting of senior leaders before the rest of management will embrace and support them.

CEOs are responsible for nurturing the overall enterprise capability mix, and rely on functional managers to supervise categories of capabilities – funds, people, and technology – and on area managers to deploy these resources and capabilities effectively. The additional owner of this challenge is the HR executive, who must develop and execute the right workforce objectives, policies, strategies and practices. In the process of coordinating the enterprise's HR objectives and strategy with its overall business strategy, HR executives must provide expert, informed and practical counsel to the CEO and executive team on all aging workforce matters. They must oversee the redesign and execution of the processes of employee recruiting, development, administration and retention to achieve preset aging workforce objectives. In short, the HR staff maintains and develops the organization's human capital to provide the necessary talent capabilities timeously and spatially in the enterprise.

In view of the imminent workforce demographic pressures, HR executives today must do more than ensure the cost-effective execution of their practices and processes. *First*, to anticipate and implement necessary changes in HR management practices, they must anticipate and assess how workforce composition and employee preferences are changing. *Second*, they must be fully aware of the different requirements for synchronization of workforce and business strategies. As the nature of work has grown more information intensive, more technically demanding, and more complex, the relative value of skills and talent in the business capability portfolio has steadily risen.

New workforce objectives, strategy and practices must become a bigger part of business strategy. This requirement becomes acute as companies now face an imminent period of workforce and skill shortages. The HR executive must articulate how the aging composition of the enterprise's workforce will enable or impede business success, and how to handle it through clear objectives and strategic actions.

Ensuring the enterprise's workforce talent and human capability supply is a responsibility that rests primarily on the CEO and the HR executive, but which is shared broadly across the enterprise. The CEO shares responsibility locally with every general manager and any manager responsible for the entire mix of business capabilities – funds, facilities, people, networking and technology. Each general manager must understand the changing composition of the workforce and how those changes influence business performance, and how they can best contribute to the identification, flow, experience, and skills of workforce resources across the enterprise. In addition, the HR executive shares responsibility across the HR function in general, and also with managers affiliated with particular business units, major business functions, and general managers in the enterprise.

The Particular Types of Business Model Objectives that are Necessary

The range and types of objectives required to respond effectively to the aging workforce challenges are best illustrated by looking at each of the four key elements (Figure 3.1) of an enterprise's business model (BM).

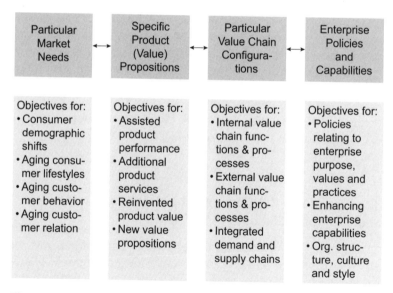

Figure 3.1
Objectives for the aging workforce in each element of an enterprise's business model (BM)

The First Key BM Element: Objectives Concerning Particular Market Needs

Understanding the shifts in consumer demographics due to an aging society will enable an enterprise to devise particular objectives concerning the shifting composition and needs of an aging enterprise workforce target market. Within an aging society, consumer lifestyles are changing, customer behavior reflects aging patterns, and customer relations' needs are consequently changing. The question is: *How can we leverage changing demographics to strengthen relationships with our customers?*

Employees are more than just work performers – they are the enterprise's face to the marketplace, especially in such sectors as retail, services, and the media. An enterprise's workforce – and not just those on the "front line" – often displays a mirror image of the ethnicity, gender, and age composition of the enterprise's evolving customer base, thereby increasing customer retention and business volume.

In retailing, for example, as the population in general ages and mature consumers exercise a greater proportion of spending power in society, retail enterprises could effectively show a more mature face to their clientele. Retailers could also increasingly recruit employees to reflect the ethnic diversity of their local markets and customers. Important questions to address are: How well do our workforce demographics correspond with our customer demographics? Do they mirror the distribution and diversity of age, ethnicities and lifestyles of customers? How can we improve and capitalize on that match?

The Second Key BM Element: Objectives Concerning Specific Product Propositions

Changing consumer demographics have significant impacts on an enterprise's product propositions – the combination of physical and intangible value provided to target markets. Product performance – be it in speed, strength, reliability or consistency – needs to be tailored to an aging consumer base. Product services provided by an aging workforce often need to be expanded to incorporate changing physical handling, utilization and storage needs of aging consumers. Objectives are necessary for reinvention of product value related to aging consumer requirements. Moreover, the business opportunities emerging from new value propositions due to aging consumers are significant, and *every enterprise should set clear objectives for new product propositions – both incremental and disruptive – focused on the aging profiles of target consumer markets.*

The Third Key BM Element: Objectives for Particular Value Chain Configurations

Enterprises usually research the design, produce/manufacture, and market & deliver products through a combination of internal organizational processes and external value chain partners. With the increase of outsourcing practices of enterprises in the past two decades, the external value chain partners of an enterprise have become extensive and widespread. Consequently, in a global networked world, the management integrated demand and supply chains, together with internal value chains of enterprises, have become a key managerial requirement.

The aging workforce has an impact not only on internal value chains, but also on external value chains. Thus, *objectives for man-*

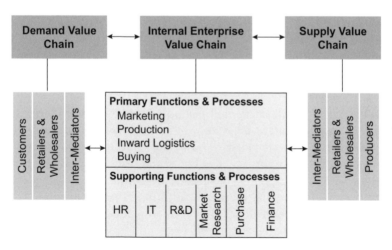

Figure 3.2
Areas of objectives for the aging workforce in generic enterprise value chain configurations

aging the aging workforce have to be set on a coordinated basis: for in-
ternal value chain functions and processes, for external value chain
functions and processes, and for integrated demand and supply chains.
Many companies that are dependent on extended supply and/or
demand chains, such as Dell, and largely virtual companies, acting as value coordinators (such as virtual wine companies), face
significant challenges in managing the implications of an aging
workforce not directly under their control.

Figure 3.2 illustrates the concept of integrated/configured value
chains and the areas in which particular objectives concerning
the managing of the aging workforce are required.

The Fourth Key BM Element: Objectives Concerning Particular Enterprise Policies and Capabilities

Every enterprise should have the objective to put policies in
place concerning the enterprise's purpose, values and practices in
an aging society, including its aging workforce. The generic purpose of making a meaningful difference in society, and to the
well-being of its workforce and the values of being a caring, nurturing, and sharing entity in external and internal practices, is especially important and needs to be explicated in particular objectives. Objectives to enhance overall and specific organizational
capabilities are crucial, especially in view of the need to sustain/
develop competitive capabilities in an innovation economy. Objectives about effective organizational structures, workplace environment, enterprise culture, and leadership and managerial
styles, concerning the aging workforce, need to be clear.

While all of the functions and processes in an enterprise's business
model are important in the context of an aging society, this book fo-
cuses more directly (and practically) on managing an enterprise's aging
workforce. For this purpose, *five key 'action fields',* as illustrated in
Figure 1.5 in Chapter 1, have been determined as crucial: enabling new managerial mindsets concerning the aging workforce;
facilitating new knowledge management processes; implementing new health management processes; adopting new human resource management (HRM) practices & tools; and facilitating appropriate work environments and physical tools for an aging
workforce. These five arenas comprise the 5V-framework to in-

crease the overall value (V) of the aging workforce of an enterprise – as detailed in Chapter 4 – and particular enterprise objectives are essential in each of these arenas.

Objectives in Each of the Five Key Organizational Action Fields

Objectives for Managerial Mindsets

A survey in the United States by Ernst & Young reported that although corporate America foresees a significant workforce shortage as boomers retire, it is not dealing well with the issue.[3] Almost three-quarters of the 1,400 global companies questioned by Deloitte in 2005 said they expected a shortage of salaried staff over the next three to five years. Yet few of them are looking to older workers to fill that shortage; and even fewer are looking to them to fill another gap that has already appeared. Many firms in Europe and America complain that they struggle to find qualified directors for their boards – this when the pool of retired from those very same firms is growing by leaps and bounds.

The question arises why enterprises are not working harder to keep older employees. *Part of the reason is that the impending aging workforce crunch has been beyond the mindsets of most managers.* Retaining older workers is not the only way to cope with a falling supply of required human resources. The participation of developing countries in the world economy has increased the overall supply – whatever the local effect of demographics is in the developed countries. An enormous amount of work is being outsourced offshore to countries such as China and India, and this likely to continue in the near future. However, the shortage is not in numbers, but in capabilities and skills, as previously highlighted.

It is important to note that legislation designed to help older workers can often act to their detriment. Contrary to its good intentions, America's Age Discrimination in Employment Act in some ways discourages the rehiring of retired workers by requiring that all employees receive equal benefits, such as health-care insurance. That is invariably more expensive for older employees, so it acts as a deterrent to hiring them. Similar legislation is likely to be enacted in Britain during late 2006, following an EU directive compelling member states to outlaw discrimination on the grounds of age.

Despite favorable changes in the relevant laws, older workers must still contend with entrenched and often hostile attitudes at work. Many people assume that older employees are less motivated, take more sick leave, and cost more for the enterprise to employ. The increasing evidence, however, is that many people over 65 have much value-added to offer, even if they are no longer at their peak (see Table 2.1). Some studies show that the over-40s are less likely to be off sick and are more highly motivated and productive (except where great physical effort is required), depending of course also on factors such as enterprise culture and management style.

Particular objectives for mindset change concerning the aging workforce are:

- Viewing older workers as valuable, with enterprise-critical skills.

- Older employees are equally motivated and enthusiastic as younger workers, with the right health, work environment, and human resource management tools.

- The wisdom and experience of older workers are important, in combination with younger talents, for innovation and business growth.

- Older workers are an investment for the future and to be nurtured, not a cost factor or a burden.

Objectives for New Knowledge Management Processes

Given that most societies are geared for retirement of workers at around age 60 to 65, enterprises face a significant challenge of knowledge management. In essence, it concerns the potential loss of valuable intellectual and skill capital. A survey of human resources directors by IBM in 2005 concluded: "When the baby-boomer generation retires, many companies will find out too late that a career's worth of experience has walked out the door, leaving insufficient talent to fill the void."[4]

In some industries and types of enterprises, this shortage seems particularly serious. In aerospace and defence, for example, as much as 40% of the workforce in some major companies will be eligible to retire within the next five years. At the same time, it is generally known that the number of engineering graduates in developed countries is in steep decline.

Particular knowledge management objectives for the aging workforce are:

• Retaining all enterprise-valuable knowledge, i.e. prevention of the loss of knowledge to the enterprise upon departure.

• Enabling existing knowledge residing in the talents, skills and capabilities of the aging workforce to remain sharp, focused and active.

• Mining the knowledge of aging workers through an appropriate enterprise knowledge management system.

• Transferring the knowledge of an aging workforce to others in the enterprise through appropriate structures (e.g. teams) and practices.

• Recovering lost knowledge in critical enterprise arenas.

• Integrating both explicit and tacit knowledge management objectives.

Objectives for Age-Related Health Management Processes

In today's world, with increasing human longevity due to scientific and medical advances, an older workforce can remain healthier and more energetic with the right enterprise approaches and practices. Particular objectives need to be put in place, such as:

• *Mental health objectives:* Mental stimulation, neurological interventions, increased diversity of roles and interesting functions and activities, and greater linkage to meaningful contributions to the purpose of the enterprise are important areas of mental health objectives for an aging workforce.

- *Physical health objectives:* Targeted physical capabilities, preventive treatment of age-related mobility impediments, regular internal medical check-ups and treatments, and physical rejuvenation targets are important areas of physical health objectives for an aging workforce.

- *Emotional health objectives:* Positive and high levels of individual and organizational energy; emotional stability; particular emotion targets, e.g. esteem, happiness, team-comfortability.

Objectives for Human Resources Management (HRM) Processes

Companies in continental Europe and Japan are finding it harder to separate age from seniority (and employee costs) than rivals in America and Britain. At Wal-Mart, the large American retailer, managers fresh out of college in the southern American states oversee women workers old enough to be their mothers. Ranjit de Sousa, Adecco's director of corporate development, cites one company where the average age of the managers is 35, while that of the employees who report to them is 42. If older workers want to stay in the workforce, they need to accept this reversal of the traditional hierarchy.[5]

In some businesses early retirement is institutionalized. At professional-service companies, such as law and accounting firms, partners are encouraged to move out at an early age of as young as 55, so as to encourage juniors with the promise of becoming a partner. At Deloitte, one of the world's biggest accounting firms, the official retirement age for partners – 60 years – is written into the partnership agreement. Although British law firms have a unique reward system, giving partners more or less equal shares of the profits, partners in American firms tend to earn according to performance. The American system enables older partners to stay on because they are not an unfair burden if their performance declines.

In many European countries, one of the largest obstacles is compensation. Adecco, a large global recruitment agency, says that in France and Germany 50- to 65-year-olds earn on average 60 to 70% more than 25- to 30-year-olds. In Britain, however, they earn more or less the same (Figure 3.3). That is one reason why

The burden of old age
Age-wage profiles
Earnings for 25-29 year olds = 100

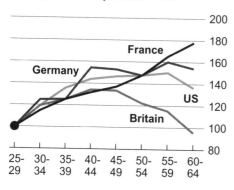

Figure 3.3
Age-wage profiles in Germany, France, USA and Britain, 2006
(Source: OECD)

more older people are employed in Britain than in Germany. In 1990 the unemployment rate among 55- to 64-year-olds in the two countries was more or less the same: 7.2% in Britain and 7.7% in Germany. By 2003, however, the rates were 3.3% and 9.7%, respectively.

The encouragement for older workers to remain at an enterprise is often a by-product of various initiatives. Many companies are cultivating a more diverse workforce, partly because legislation in some countries decrees it, and partly because they believe it can help them. Although diversity predominantly means recruiting more women and ethnic minorities, it assists older workers as well. Practical measures, such as flexible work schedules designed to encourage mothers to return to the workforce, can also encourage older workers to stay.

Older workers stand to gain from efforts to recruit younger workers in the changing knowledge-based economy. Sabri Challah, the head of Deloitte's human-capital practice, says that companies are making great efforts to recruit (and retain) the youngest cohort of workers, the 'Generation Y'. The '20-something' workers (who are entering the workforce later and staying for a shorter time with each employer) have very different attitudes to work, life, permanency and careers than their parents did. In trying to design flexible working lives for them, companies are increasingly forced to accommodate older workers as well.

In overall perspective, it is clear that enterprises need to become seriously involved with all employees about their plans for life, talents and retirement. Many have no demographic profile of their workforce and little idea about how much of it is retiring when. In America, employers are also often afraid to discuss retirement plans for fear of lawsuits under age-discrimination legislation, and this issue needs to be urgently addressed.

Particular HRM objectives for the aging workforce are:

- Ensure increased productivity, retention, and return on recruitment and training investment.

- Remove discouraging retirement practices that have become institutionalized over time.

- Adjust the enterprise reward system to encourage the aging workforce to be employed for lengthier periods of time.

- Establish a professional succession planning and clear demographic profiles of the workforce in terms of retirement expectations and requirements.

- Devise particular programs to make it more attractive and rewarding for aging workers to remain employed for longer periods of time.

- Adapt organization culture, age-related employee motivation, job diversity, flexibility and mobility.

Objectives for the Work Environment and Physical Tools for an Aging Workforce

The work environment – in terms of ergonomics such as pleasant surroundings, lifestyle-enhancing activities, and age-sensitive physical layouts – as well as physical tools to make activities easier or more convenient, play an important role in retaining an aging workforce.

Particular objectives for the aging workforce are:

- Target levels of making the workplace a pleasant, convenient place that resembles an extension of aging workforce lifestyles.

- Target levels of work flexibility, enabling workers to move around from place to place.

- Achieve targeted levels of facilitating aging workers with appropriate physical tools and protective mechanisms.

- Enable easy physical mobility between workstations and organizational artifacts: Install particular levels of physical mobility, especially in the 'digital' workplace.

From the above range of objectives in each of the five key organizational fields, it is obvious that particular actions can be designed only if such objectives are clear and integrated.

Towards Integrated Aging-Focused Workforce Objectives

Aging-focused workforce objectives should not be piecemeal or mechanistic, but integrated across internal processes and external processes, and in long-term context of demographic trends and impacts. Besides the conceptual grasp of this fact, there are technical tools to assist in aging-focused integrated workforce objectives and programs. For example, the Swiss energy firm Axpo Holding implements a computer software tool that assists to integrate all managerial competency areas with an employee demographic profile.[6]

The 5V-Scorecard presented in this book provides guidelines for individual and collective integration of age-focused workforce objectives.

Key Pointers of Chapter 3

- It is essential that an enterprise should have clear, integrated objectives to increase the value of an aging workforce. These include key enterprise value dimensions such as productivity, innovation & business growth, work processes, learning processes, culture, and management styles.

- The responsibility for setting integrated objectives is primarily with two people in the enterprise: the CEO and the head of human resources.

- The particular types of enterprise objectives that are necessary for an aging workforce can best be understood and developed when looking at the four key elements of an enterprise's business model: objectives concerning respectively particular market needs, specific product (value) propositions, particular value chain configurations, internal and external value chains, and enterprise policies and capabilities.

- Objectives should be practically outlined for each of the five key organizational action fields, i.e. managerial mindsets concerning the aging workforce, age-related knowledge management processes, age-focused health management processes, human resource management objectives, and objectives for the work environment and physical tools for an aging workforce.

- Particular tools, e.g. computer software tools, exist to assist the integration of all managerial competency areas with employee demographic profiles.

3 Company Objectives to Increase the Value (V)

4 The 5V-Framework to Increase both Productivity and Creativity of the Aging Workforce

Key Issues of this Chapter

- The two key value-adding dimensions of the workforce
- Why a 5V-framework?
- Dynamics of the 5V-framework
- Managing the 5V-framework as a process

The Two Key Value-Adding Dimensions of the Workforce in Any Enterprise

The two key value-adding dimensions of the workforce in any enterprise are increased productivity and increased creativity: *productivity* is predominantly an efficiency mechanism and measurement, concerned with either greater output for same input, or same output for less input, or ideally both; while *creativity* is the human ingenuity that is necessary to enable innovation in enterprise business models, strategies, markets, products, operations and capabilities. Existing managerial mindsets mainly consider the aging workforce as necessarily declining in productivity as aging progresses, and also that workforce creativity – for innovation and development of new enterprise value propositions – will decrease due to aging.

With an inexorable demographic reality of aging populations and workforces in especially developed countries now becoming acute, the major managerial concerns are starting to focus on how to maintain – and especially to increase – both productivity and creativity levels of an aging workforce. Success in this endeavor is evidently crucial for the future competitiveness and sustained performance of enterprises in a knowledge-networked global innovation economy.

Our research in several industries and companies has shown that there are 5 major organizational action fields that need to be focused on to increase the productivity and creativity of an aging workforce – what we call the 5V-framework.

Why a 5V-Framework?

The 5V-framework is illustrated in Figure 4.1, with subsequent motivation.

While it is important to understand the entire business model of the enterprise to consider the impacts of an aging society on its nature, purpose and networks, it is also critical to focus on the practical processes to maintain and increase both productivity and creativity of an aging workforce. The focus of this book is on managing the aging workforce in an enterprise and on the processes involved to achieve the critical objectives concerning enterprise productivity and creativity.

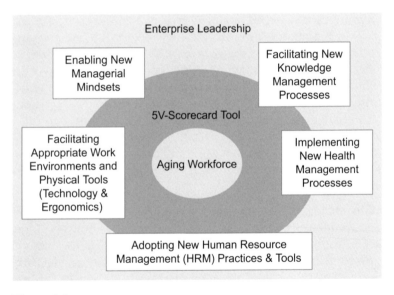

Figure 4.1
The 5V-framework – organizational action fields to manage an aging workforce

Furthermore, while a value chain approach (primary value-adding functions and supporting value-adding functions) is useful to analyze important parts of a business model, it is more appropriate to look at key enterprise processes directly affecting the performance – productivity and creativity – of an aging workforce. The 5 key organizational action fields depicted in the 5V-framework include all of the important organizational processes in a simple but powerfully effective way. The 5V-framework also has the advantage of being easy to comprehend, practical to use, and combined as an effective scorecard tool for continuous implementation and measurement.

Dynamics of the 5V-Framework

In Chapters 5 to 9 each of the five action fields of the 5V-framework are discussed in detail. Before looking at each of these in particular, it is important to understand the overall (holistic) concept and especially its interrelated dynamics. The following facts illustrate this:

- Productivity increases happen because of a range of measures: doing things right and also doing the right things. Process, product and customer efficiencies are due to doing things consistently right in knowledge management, human resource management, particular work environments and proper physical tools, and with healthy employees in their mind, bodies and emotions.

- Creativity and innovative capability are sustained and increased because of mindsets attuned to doing things different, improved or in totally new value-adding ways. Process, product and customer innovation arise due to particular knowledge environments, human resource management practices, work environments, and with healthy workers in mind, body and emotions.

- New managerial mindsets concerning the aging workforce are an important prerequisite to devise and implement appropriate knowledge management processes, and work environments and physical tools (technologies, artifacts and ergonomics).

- Knowledge management processes – both external and tacit knowledge management processes, and including knowledge retention, expansion, rejuvenation, transfer, retrieval and appropriate use – are dependent on human resources management processes, healthy attitudes and physical performance of aging employees, conducive work environments and physical facilities & tools, and organizational culture and leadership style.

- Health management processes influence the mindset, physical abilities and competencies, knowledge utilization capacities, work environments and safety procedures, and human resource management processes concerning an aging workforce. Health is not just a physical issue and concern but also a mental and emotional concern – with the increasing incidence of 'head health' ailments (and treatments) in the world, this is becoming especially important.

- Human resource management processes concerning an aging workforce are due for an immense reshaping and change. As indicated previously, extant HRM processes are still largely rooted in 20th century principles, attitudes and practices. In a knowledge-networked innovation economy, with a significantly aging workforce, the reinvented HRM functions – and processes – need to incorporate all of the other four key organizational action fields. In fact, the mindsets of HRM drivers/functionaries need to be significantly adjusted as a prerequisite for reinvention of the HRM function.

- The 5V-framework is not a mechanistic concept, i.e. it cannot be rigidly formulated and mechanistically (for example, step-by-step) applied. It is a dynamic concept with interactive processes and multiple feedback loops among actions and outcomes. However, because of the requirement of responsibility to be assigned for implementing the 5V-Scorecard (see Chapter 10), it is useful to consider the HRM function as the main intervenor/coordinator and measurer of managerial processes aimed at the aging workforce.

- Enterprise leadership and management at all levels have the task to enable, introduce, facilitate and help implement actions for an aging workforce to sustain and increase levels of productivity and innovation in the enterprise.

- The theory of constraints (TOC) is based on the reality that a dynamic system is only as good as its weakest link. If any of the five key actions arenas is weak, the entire 5V system will be negatively affected.[1]

Managing the 5V-Framework as a Process

The following process to manage the 5V concept and dynamic framework is recommended:

1. Understand the basic business model of your enterprise and the likely impacts of an aging society, and especially the aging workforce, on its business model.

2. Identify the core value-adding processes in the enterprise and their respective impacts on enterprise productivity and creativity.

3. Use a simple matrix (see below) to jointly view the five organizational action fields and the identified core processes in (2).

4. Apply the 5V-Scorecard (detailed in Chapter 10) to measure the impacts and/or results or actions taken in each of the five action fields.

The above-mentioned process needs to be introduced and driven by enterprise leadership, which is required to assign responsibilities for particular actions and measurements. Managing the aging workforce is such a crucial issue for the future survival and performance of an enterprise that the overall responsibility for this process cannot be delegated only to the HRM function or any other enterprise function – it should be guided, driven and measured by enterprise leadership, especially the CEO and/or the executive team.

Table 4.1 illustrates a process-action matrix to assist in managing the 5V-framework as a process. For each field of the matrix, all relevant actions may be defined.

Table 4.1
Implementation matrix for action fields linked to core enterprise processes

		CORE ENTERPRISE PROCESSES				
		Marketing	R & D	Production	Logistics & Distribution	New Business Development
ACTION FIELDS FOR AGING WORK-FORCE	Managerial Mindsets					
	Knowledge Management					
	Health Management					
	HRM					
	Workplace Environment & Tools					

The matrix shown does not include the measurement of the impact of the five action field interventions on the aging workforce – these are illustrated in Chapter 10, i.e. the measurement of the impact of interventions on enterprise productivity and creativity.

Key Pointers of Chapter 4

- In view of the significant demographic shifts in the workforce, any enterprise should be concerned about the potential impact on the two key value-adding (and competitive-critical) dimensions: productivity (for increased efficiency) and creativity (for increased innovation).

- It is critically important to discern practical fields of managerial intervention to influence enterprise processes for both productivity and innovation goals. The 5V-framework recommended in this chapter is based on our extensive business research, and comprises 5 key organizational action fields.

4 The 5V-Framework

- The 5V-framework is a dynamic concept (or model), not a mechanistic, step-by-step formula process. The five action fields are interactive with multiple feedback loops and cross-impacts.

- While the HRM function in an enterprise could fulfill some responsibilities as coordinator and measurer of impacts, overall leadership and management in the various enterprise areas should enable, introduce, facilitate, and help implement actions for an aging workforce.

- To assist in managing the 5V-framework as a process, a simple implementation matrix for action fields linked to core enterprise process is recommended.

PART III

The Five Value-Adding Fields

5 The First V-Field: Mindset Change Approaches for the Aging Workforce

Key Issues of this Chapter

- The prerequisite: understanding the mature worker
- The necessity of a new managerial mindset concerning the aging workforce
- Key elements of a new managerial mindset about the aging workforce
- Enabling a new managerial mindset to be embedded in the organization
- Approaches to manage mindsets change processes, both internally and externally to the enterprise

The Prerequisite: Understanding the Mature Worker

Older workers, whether they are 45, 60 or 70, are usually the victims of outdated attitudes, stereotyping, unfair policies, biases and prejudices. This can negatively affect older workers by e.g.:

- Premature termination of their services
- Denying them promotions
- Excluding them from learning and training opportunities
- Neglecting appropriate rewards for their performance.

Beliefs and "myths", whether right or wrong, about the value-added contributions, health conditions, safety requirements, mobility and effectiveness of older workers may influence whether they are hired, retained, repositioned, or job-terminated through e.g. retrenchment, firing or other methods. A common misperception is that older workers are burdens to a work environment, rigidly set in their ways, "over the hill", and cannot work safely and effectively. Not only can these mistaken beliefs harm older workers, they also negatively affect employers and businesses, particularly since older workers are a valuable human resource in any labor market, and especially in the labor markets of today.

The following chart presents and responds to some of these myths:[1]

Myths and Realities about Older Workers

Myth	Reality
Older workers are more likely to have work-related injuries.	Not true. In fact, older workers suffer fewer job-related injuries.
Older people are all alike.	Differences within age groups, especially in the more mature ones, are often greater than those between age groups.
Older adults are unable or unwilling to learn new processes or skills.	Age does not determine curiosity or the willingness to learn. Older workers may sometimes take slightly longer to learn certain tasks and may respond better to training methods more suited to their needs.
Older adults avoid new approaches or new technologies.	Many people, regardless of age, enjoy new technology. There is e.g. an increased internet usage of people over 50 years, especially in online partner search agencies as well as in chat forums. Older workers are likely to respond well to innovation if it: • relates to what they already know, • allows for self-paced learning, • provides opportunities for practice and support.
Older workers have failing memories.	Long-term memory continues to increase with age. Contextual intelligence, i.e. intelligence based on experience over the life course of employees, is stable or even slightly increases.

Myth	Reality
It is not worthwhile investing in training older workers because they are likely to leave or are "just coasting to retirement."	Older workers tend to be loyal and less likely to change jobs frequently. This is particularly the case if older workers know their efforts are appreciated and they are not faced with a mandatory retirement age.
	One Canadian survey showed that 21.4 percent of workers 45 and over planned to never retire or retire after 65.
	A more recent survey by Ipsos Reid in December 2005, conducted for the Bank of Montreal, found that 58 percent of the (Canadian) pre-retirees surveyed planned on working for an employer in some capacity following traditional retirement.
	In a knowledge economy, the payback period on investment in training is becoming shorter for all workers. That means that spending on training older workers is very likely to be recovered before these workers retire.
Older workers are less productive.	Productivity is individual and varies more within an age group than between age groups. No significant impact on productivity due to aging is likely until workers are well into their 70s.
	Older workers may be less productive doing heavy physical work. However, most jobs do not require maximum physical exertion. Older workers generally make up for any decline in physical or mental ability through experience and forethought. If strength and agility are a factor, older workers can usually find ways to compensate by "working smarter."
	Older workers are often well trained and have a track record of responsibility and dedication.
Older workers relate poorly to customers.	Older workers can often be more effective than younger workers when experience or people skills are needed, as when dealing with customers or building a client base.

5 The First V-Field: Mindset Change Approaches

Myth	Reality
Older workers are inflexible.	Older workers may be more cautious, a trait that can improve accuracy and safety.
Older adults have impaired mental or intellectual capacity.	Studies show that intellectual abilities stay intact into the 70s and beyond. Short-term memory may start declining well before age 45, crystallized intelligence, i.e. intelligence for learning new things (e.g. new computer languages), even starts declining with approximately 25 years, but measurable, in-depth knowledge continues to increase as we age. Age tends to enhance the ability to perform activities depending on judgment, decision-making and general knowledge.
Most older adults have poor health.	Three-quarters of Canadians aged 65 to 74 and two-thirds of those over 75 rate their health as good or very good. These figures are even higher for workers aged 45 to 64.
Older workers are more likely to suffer from illness and are more often absent or late for work than younger workers.	True is that some studies, especially the ones conducted in the industries that require physically intensive labor, such as the automotive and steel industry, show that sick leave cases remain stable over different age cohorts. Absolute sick leave days increase with age as older employees require longer times of absence to recover than younger ones. Nevertheless, most studies show older workers have lower absenteeism and tend to be more punctual than younger workers. Usually, older workers with health conditions requiring extensive sick leave have left the workforce on their own accord. Any significant increase in hospital stays or sick leaves is not likely to show up until people are over 80.
Older workers have less education.	While this may have been true at one time, it is less a factor now when many well-educated baby boomers fill the ranks of older workers.

Sometimes workers are described according to four so-called 'generations' they belong to, according to their birth-era's:

- Pre-boomers or mature/silent generation, born before 1946
- Baby-boomers, born during the years of 1946 to 1964
- Generation Xers, born during the years of 1964 to 1981
- Generation Yers, born since 1981.

The following chart shows workplace attitudes and behavior that have sometimes been linked to these four generations:[2]

Pre-boomer/mature/silent generation	• Long tenure with organizations • Respect hierarchies and authority figures • Like structure and rules • Demonstrate strong work ethic • Pay attention to the quality of work • Less mobility between jobs
Baby-boomers	• Skeptical of authority figures • Results-driven and ambitious • Have long-term aspirations with organizations • Retain what they learn • Idealistic and competitive • People-focused • Generally optimistic
Generation X	• Comfortable with diversity • Value freedom and informality • Have short-term loyalty • Work well in networks and teams • Embrace technology • Seek life-work balance • Learn quickly • Generally skeptical
Generation Y	• Comfortable with diversity • Value informality • Have short-term loyalty • Learn quickly • Embrace technology • Need supervision

It is important to realize that those born in the same year or belonging to the same generation are of course not all alike. However, some of these shared characteristics explain how workers from the same generation approach work and communicate with co-workers and supervisors.

Generational differences are often reflected in:

- Workers' attitudes to and expectations of work
- Methods of communication
- Attitudes toward authority
- Approaches to learning
- Agility in performing activities
- Acceptance of new methods and practices.

Such different approaches and attitudes may sometimes influence how workers view or react, e.g. to workplace health and safety advice. For example, older workers with a strong work ethic and commitment to their workplace and employer may consider it prudent to neglect personal situations, and turn up for work even if they are tired or sick. However, a worker with influenza could infect co-workers and a tired worker could risk their own and others' safety. Employers and supervisors should be sensitive to, and ready to respond to, such potential generational differences in attitude.

Positive Qualities of Older Workers

Negative myths and stereotypes about older workers are generally untrue, and the reality is that hiring and retaining older workers offer many advantages. In general, *some of the major positive qualities that older workers bring to the job include:*

- A strong work ethic
- Reliability and a proven performance record
- Confident knowledge, skills and capabilities
- A sense of responsibility, conscientiousness and duty to the job

- Loyalty and commitment to the organization

- Less likelihood of switching jobs

- A co-operative and team-oriented attitude

- An ability to work with different people

- Access to a wide range of community contacts – especially important in sales and marketing

- Wisdom and an ability to serve as role models and mentors

- Life and work experience

- Lower absenteeism in some industries and businesses (especially in non-physical labor intensive industries).

The Necessity of a New Managerial Mindset Concerning the Aging Workforce

Not only a new managerial mindset about the aging workforce arises from an understanding of the mature worker, but also how to deal with them effectively. Wrong managerial mental models exist concerning careers, roles and schedules, and what mature workers want from their employers. De Long mentions six problems, or "mistakes", that are crippling organizational efforts due to the lack of appropriate managerial mindsets concerning the aging workforce:[3]

Problem #1

Assuming leaders will proactively and effectively implement solutions once aging workforce threats become crucial

Some companies are good at diagnosing where they are most vulnerable to losing employees with critical knowledge. However, when it comes to proactively implementing specific solutions, such as accelerated mentoring programs, investing in knowledge capture systems, or hiring successors early enough to train them, leaders are often reluctant to provide the political support or the resources needed. *The development of executives that are aware, oriented and able to proactively deal with these challenges should be an essential part of every aging workforce initiative.*

Problem #2

Inability to relate aging workforce challenges and solutions to the enterprise's strategic objectives

Managers in one large aerospace company undertook a major knowledge retention initiative when the firm began losing too many engineers with specialized knowledge needed to maintain one type of aircraft they had built. But company executives terminated the project a year later because it was not delivering results that were clearly linked to business outcomes. Retaining and developing workforce capabilities must always be connected to enterprise and managerial objectives. *Building a clear enterprise strategy case for knowledge retention is the only way to overcome the inevitable conflicts that arise when internal and external business needs start competing for the same capabilities.*

Problem #3

Regarding partial or 'quick-fix' solutions as adequate

The threat of losing 20 to 50 percent of an enterprise's employees in the next five years is a sobering situation. But the solution does not lie in one or two initiatives applied uniformly across the organization. Implementing a new succession planning process or implementing a flexible phased retirement program won't be adequate for creating an adequate future workforce when significant experience is leaving in a short period of time. *Companies need an integrated portfolio of solution-options that can be customized to meet the requirements of individual units and departments.* Responding to the knowledge retention needs of R&D scientists, for example, is different than meeting the requirements for effective senior management succession.

Problem #4

Neglecting employee attitudes concerning the sharing of valuable knowledge

Employees often have a wide range of feelings about sharing knowledge. In organizations like NASA and the World Bank, where there is a strong commitment to the organization's ongoing mission, veteran workers are more likely to willingly share what they have learned. In many firms today, employees who feel burned out and cynical because of past layoffs and budget cuts, are likely to be unmotivated to participate in knowledge sharing programs. *It is important to ascertain employees' actual level of commitment when designing knowledge retention strategies, for management to ensure that new programs and systems are aligned with peoples' willingness to cooperate.*

Problem #5

Overestimating technology solutions to "capture" knowledge

Sandia Labs spent millions of dollars videotaping hundreds of employees who were about to retire. Unfortunately, it turned out younger workers at the nuclear weapons lab were not interested in reviewing hours of video tape to find some useful pointers from an aging worker, no matter how smart he or she was. The business world is already full of unused "lessons learned" databases and videotapes created with departing employees. In the area of knowledge retention, overestimating technology solutions as a means of capturing knowledge is a recipe for failure. Of course, *technology has an important role to play in supporting knowledge retention efforts, but it must be applied in alignment with existing enterprise knowledge sharing and learning behaviors and practices.*

Problem #6

Inadequate coordination of aging workforce solutions

There is a wide range of initiatives available to support the development of future workforce capabilities, to compensate for attrition among highly skilled employees. Most enterprises are not effectively coordinating these efforts, and the opportunity costs are tremendous. *Strengthening an enterprise's workforce to attain strate-*

gic objectives means coordinating and integrating activities in a number of areas:

(1) Human resources policies and processes, such as succession planning and phased retirement practices

(2) The use of a variety of knowledge transfer and recovery practices, such as documentation, storytelling, re-contracting, mentoring and coaching

(3) Leveraging IT applications effectively to support knowledge capture, sharing, and reuse

(4) The physical work environment and positioning, use and redesigning of tools

(5) Health management in a holistic sense, including the physical, mental and emotional health of workers

Urgency to Change the Status Quo

The challenges posed by an aging workforce, and linked to that increasing employee turnover and skill shortages, are now beginning to gather greater management attention. Much more urgency and focused attention are necessary, however, because there will be staggering capability deficiencies in the immediate years ahead due to the departure of experienced managers and professionals from enterprises throughout the developed world. Industry and enterprise performances are clearly facing a major challenge in the near future, and how leaders and managers proactively gear themselves for this will be crucial.

Key Elements of a New Managerial Mindset about the Aging Workforce

Employees of all ages desire meaningful work and responsibility, opportunities to learn, a congenial and respectful workplace, fair pay, and adequate benefits. Aging workers expect such a mix, especially elements such as pension accumulation and payout options, to reflect the value of their experience and their retirement preferences. *The aging workforce's need for respect and appropriate work environment, and especially learning opportunities, are most often neglected by enterprises.*

Table 5.1 shows, based on research studies, what older workers desire most – in ranked order of relative importance – among ten basic elements of the "employment deal."[4] Not surprisingly, a comprehensive retirement package heads the list, followed by a comprehensive benefits package (with emphasis on health-care coverage). The subsequent several elements involve the work experience. Older workers value the conditions for personal contribution, enjoyment, and growth more highly than work arrangements (flexible schedule and location) and more than significant increases in compensation and vacation. Note that more money and vacation matter least to older workers, partly because they are probably well paid already and have earned longer vacations.

This pattern – valuing security highest, work and workplace next, and the work arrangement and compensation lowest – recurs in the other worker cohorts, but it's most pronounced among older workers.

Table 5.1
Employment deal elements ranked by older workers
(relative weights add to 100)

General elements of the employment deal	Relative weight
Comprehensive retirement package	16
Comprehensive benefits package	14
Work that enables me to learn and grow	13
Work that is personally stimulating	12
Workplace that is enjoyable	11
Flexible work schedule	8
Work that is worthwhile to society	8
Ten percent more in total compensation	7
Flexible workplace	6
Two weeks' additional paid vacation	5

5 The First V-Field: Mindset Change Approaches

A "career path" is traditionally viewed as a straight line or a climb up the "corporate ladder" of responsibility and rank that plummets suddenly at retirement. That is now becoming entirely the wrong mental model for an extended career in today's workforce environment. As previously indicated, people desire to adjust their roles, schedules, and other work arrangements as they approach retirement. They want change relatively into a less intensive but still rewarding work pattern that can evolve through and past any official age of retirement, thereby continuing to make a significant value-added contribution to the enterprise's future performance.

The key elements of a new managerial mindset are:

- *Firstly*, older employees want to contribute meaningfully, potentially assuming leadership positions relatively late in their careers and bridging leadership gaps during organizational transitions. *Management must not overlook the leadership potential of "late bloomers."*

- *Second*, like workers of all ages, older workers want to continue improving their skills and expanding their talents, but companies continually overlook them for training and development, when traditional retirement is nearing on the horizon. For example, in Germany 95% of all employees – according to Eurostat – do not get any training and from 45 years onwards hardly any do. This is a major mistake, since staff turnover tends to be lowest among older employees, and the return on the educational investment in older workers can therefore be higher than on an equivalent investment in younger employees. *To expand the contribution of these experienced workers, enterprises should engage them as trainers, coaches, and mentors, instead of merely contracting them occasionally as outside consultants.*

- *Third*, flexible work arrangements – such as flexible work schedules – will become more important as the proportion of older workers increases. *Flexibility must be a part of the employment deal both as workers phase into retirement and as retirees return to work, and management should quickly master the practices of flexible work and flexible retirement.*

Enabling a New Managerial Mindset to be Embedded in the Organization

To enable a new managerial mindset concerning the aging workforce to become embedded in the organization, the following policy measures should be adopted:

- *Discard age bias in hiring older workers*

  Although some countries have already banned discrimination against older workers, age bias persists in many organizations. The examples in the box show how some companies are dealing with age bias.[5]

Age Bias and How Some Companies are Dealing with It

Age bias can surface in the wording of a simple job advertisement. "High energy", "fast pace", and "fresh thinking" communicate "youth wanted here", whereas "experience", "knowledge", and "expertise" say "we value maturity." Recruiting channels such as newspaper want ads, "help wanted" signs, or the various job-listing websites may not attract older workers. Instead, travel programs for older adults (like Elderhostel), senior centers, country clubs, and retirement communities can all serve as productive recruiting venues. For example, CVS pharmacy store chain in the U.S. looked at national demographic trends fifteen years ago and concluded that it needed to employ far more older workers. But managers didn't know how to find them – older people shopped in CVS stores but didn't apply for openings. Now the company works through the National Council on the Aging, Experience Works, AARP, city agencies, and community organizations to locate productive new employees.

Candidate screening and interviewing techniques can unintentionally put off mature candidates as well. People accustomed to more traditional approaches to demonstrating their skills may balk at having to build something with Lego or explain how M&Ms are made. One major British bank realized that its psychometric and verbal-reasoning tests intimidated older candidates, and so it used role-playing exercises instead to gauge candidates' ability to handle customers. Britain's largest building society, Nationwide, has begun short-listing job candi-

---

dates through telephone interviews to reduce the number of applicants rejected simply because they look older.

- *Create a culture that embraces older workers and honors experience*

Older workers will be attracted to a culture that values their experience and capabilities – an environment that will take some time to build, but essential to embed in all areas of the enterprise.[6] The following box indicates how some companies have been embedding such a culture.

How Some Companies are Creating a Culture that Embraces Older Workers and Honors Experience

The *Aerospace Corporation* is a company that has, over the years, built a reputation for valuing experience and knowledge. Nearly half of its 3,400 regular, full-time employees are over age 50 – a clear signal to job candidates that experience is appreciated. *CVS* also has made great strides in creating a company that has more than doubled the percentage of employees over age 50 in the past 12 years. It has no mandatory retirement age, making it easy to join the company at an advanced age and stay indefinitely (six employees are in their nineties). The company boosts its age-friendly image through internal and external publications. Company and Human Resources Department (HRD) newsletters highlight the productivity and effectiveness of older workers, and the company co-produces with a cosmetics company a senior-focused magazine that's called *In Step with Healthy Living*.

At *Dow Chemical*, the company-wide expectation is that employees at all levels will continue to learn and grow; as a result, employees regularly seek training and development opportunities, readying themselves for their next career moves.

- *Offer flexible work*

Companies need to design jobs in such ways that staying on is more attractive than leaving. Many older workers want to keep working but in a less time-consuming and pressured capacity so that they may pursue other interests.[7] Many baby-boomers also have a direct and compelling need for flexibility to accommodate multiple commitments, such as caring for children and elderly parents at the same time. "Flexiwork" – flexible in both where and when work is performed, as well as flexibility in the traditional career path – can offer many attractions and rewards and appeal to employees' changing needs. Enterprises that have successful flexiwork programs not only make these programs easily accessible to older workers, but also structure them so that people who participate don't feel that they're being sidelined or neglected for promotions – flexible types of participation should lead to a win-win situation for both employer and employee.

- *Offer flexible retirement*

  Some companies are starting to design flexible retirement models in which employees can continue to contribute in some fashion – to their own satisfaction and to the company's benefit.[8] Some regulations currently restrict workers from effectively moving in and out of flexible work arrangements. In the U.S., the IRS prohibits defined benefit plans from making distributions until formal employment ends, or an employee reaches "normal" retirement age. Furthermore, pension calculations often discourage people even from reducing their hours with a current employer prior to retirement, because payouts are often determined by the rate of pay in the last few years of work.

  From the viewpoint of the employee, flexiwork programs offer opportunities to mix work and other pursuits. They also offer personal fulfillment and growth, ongoing financial rewards, and continued enjoyment of collegial interactions. For employers, the programs provide an elastic pool of staff on demand and an on-call corps of experienced people who can work part-time as the business needs them.

- *Utilize and publicize the benefits of an aging workforce inside and outside the enterprise*

  A powerful way to enable a new managerial mindset of an aging workforce to be embedded in the organization is through the widespread demonstration effects of its benefits. Six important benefits should be publicized:

  a) The mentoring impacts and results of experienced mature workers for younger employees in the organization.

b) The benefits of the services of key employees and top performers who might otherwise join competitors. They could be assigned new responsibilities or reduced hours instead of full retirement.

c) Retain and transfer institutional, industry, project, and customer knowledge and expertise, as older employees remain longer with the enterprise.

d) Provide highly experienced temporary talent pools, and thus moderate fluctuations in staffing needs without utilizing traditional employment agencies or incurring recruiting costs.

e) Utilize leadership talent to fill unexpected gaps, facilitate executive transitions, and groom the next generation of leaders for eventual succession. Retirees can act as 'mentors on demand' and help to maintain the leadership pipeline.

f) Benefits of cost advantages, by getting the same skilled labor at equivalent salary levels but saving on the costs of benefits – not just healthcare, but pension contributions, vacation time, and others.

Tools to Manage Mindset Change Processes both Internally and Externally to the Enterprise

Although mindsets should primarily be changed among managers and employees within an organization, there are also various external stakeholders such as government, suppliers, distributors, industry associations, and even customer groups that need to be influenced through various methods or tools.

The major tools are:

- *Lobbying tools to change laws, regulations and conventions*
  Governmental legislation concerning age discrimination, health treatment for the aged, revenue and tax regimes, and industry conventions need to be influenced by lobbying and negotiating mechanisms.

- *Managerial employee-engagement tools*

Engaged workers are more productive and contribute positively to financial success. For many companies, improving engagement and job involvement is undoubtedly one of the single most powerful levers available to improve managerial mindsets and increase organizations' mental energy.[9] Customization of the employee experience – including the nature of the work itself, management style, as well as components of compensation – is feasible, practical, and the key to improving effective older worker engagement.

Employee-engagement is much more than simple satisfaction with the employment arrangements or basic loyalty to the employer – characteristics that most companies have traditionally measured and managed. Although employee satisfaction and engagement often go together, they're different phenomena arising from different sources. Employee satisfaction is about sufficiency – enough pay, benefits, and flexibility to work and live meaningfully, and no major problems or sense of unfair treatment to sour one's attitude toward the employer.

Employee engagement, in contrast, is about passion and commitment – the willingness to invest personal time and expend one's discretionary effort to help the enterprise succeed. For engaged employees, time passes quickly because they identify with the task at hand, resist distractions, spread their enthusiasm to others, and care deeply about the results.

The costs of low employee-engagement are generally regarded as enormous. Such costs accumulate quickly as people do the minimum necessary and withhold the discretionary behaviors – insight, originality, judgment, humor, leadership, proactive innovation – that enables a high-performance organization to sustain itself. Managerial employee-engagement activities – the ability of managers to connect with individual employees in meaningful ways – are a critically important element in changing mindsets about the aging workforce.

- *Demonstration-effect tools*

The use of enterprise and organizational case examples in seminars, training sessions, teamwork and other instances, serve as powerful demonstration-effect tools – in holding up a mirror of what has been happening at other enterprises or in the organization itself in the past. Managers relate strongly to other companies having similar challenges, what they have implemented and how it has worked for them. The "ah-hah" factor, or the "light-bulb switching on" factor, is an illustration of mindset changes due to powerful associations.

- *Project team diversity tools*

  Mindset changes often occur when people from diverse backgrounds – in age, experience, activities and mindsets – are put together in project teams.[10] They are forced to discuss various options to achieve solutions to problems or challenges, and mindsets are often changed in such settings. It is necessary to put together project teams consisting of younger, middle-aged and mature workers to enable mindset changes to be effected.

- *Aging workforce debriefing tools*

  Subsequent to the implementation of new aging workforce focused policy measures – such as creating a culture that honors experience and offering flexible work options and flexible retirement options – managerial debriefing sessions to illustrate the impact thereof on enterprise performance will serve as a powerful mechanism for mindset change.

Key Pointers of Chapter 5

- The major prerequisite to devise and implement managerial mindset change tools is an excellent understanding of the mature worker. This will dispel entrenched myths and traditional stereotypes of the aging workforce and provide a thorough grasp of the realities and appropriate views.

- Six common problems, or constraints, are crippling organizational efforts due to the lack of appropriate managerial mindsets about the aging workforce. These constraints must be removed to obtain a new mindset about the aging workforce.

- The key elements of a new managerial mindset about the aging workforce are: discarding of age bias in hiring mature workers; creating a culture that embraces older workers and honors experience; offering flexible work opportunities; offering flexible retirement options; and publicization of the benefits of an aging workforce due to practical experience.

- Tools to manage mindset change processes include: lobbying tools; managerial employee-engagement tools; demonstration-effect tools; project team diversity tools; and aging workforce debriefing tools.

5 The First V-Field: Mindset Change Approaches

6 The Second V-Field: Knowledge Management (KM) Approaches for the Aging Workforce

Key Issues of this Chapter

- Understanding the nature of knowledge threats to the enterprise due to the aging workforce
- A practical KM model for an aging workforce
- How to retain critical knowledge: a knowledge-retention framework and actions
- How to transfer tacit knowledge, wisdom and "deep smarts" of an aging workforce
- Knowledge-recovery initiatives
- KM and overall enterprise sustainability: the systemic context of the aging workforce

Understanding the Nature of Knowledge Threats to the Enterprise Due to the Aging Workforce

In any enterprise, the processes of knowledge generation, transfer, learning, retention and recovery serve as the basis for creating and generating human capital and adding value for the organization.

Older workers possess essential knowledge capabilities and competencies, organizational and technical experience, and problem identification and solution expertise. Explicit, implicit and tacit knowledge is at risk of being lost or depleted when older workers leave an organization. Consequently, enterprise strategies and practices that facilitate retention, transfer and use of all types of critical knowledge are critical competitive advantages for successful enterprises.

Older workers do not only possess knowledge, but they also possess organizational capabilities and wisdom. Understanding the nature and development of wisdom is the focus of much psychological and interdisciplinary research.[1] Wisdom is often viewed as possessing expert knowledge, and it also incorporates more general (or wider) knowledge, beliefs, and values about conducting a life that is balanced, meaningful and positive. We view wisdom as a capability and practice that is embedded in everyday work application and practice – wisdom therefore includes knowledge, insight, judgment and practice that are generated and transmitted at the 'boundaries' between functions, organizations and professions, i.e. between groups and individuals, and even between generations.[2]

The major impacts of the expected "brain exodus" (or "brain drain") due to demographic trends and their impacts will be felt soon, primarily between 2007 and 2015, according to the U.S. General Accounting Office Study on Older Workers.[3] Thus, the reality for most enterprises is that they will experience a "brain exodus" over the next several years as the first wave of "Baby-Boomers" (born in 1946) retire at age 60 from 2006. This is expected to have a significant impact on enterprises' capabilities to survive and flourish.

New approaches, systems and actions are needed to meet this challenge before the critical knowledge, wisdom and "deep smarts" (embedded know-how) leave organizations. Japan is a country that is likely to be in the forefront of demographic changes impacting on its knowledge base, as evidenced in several key reports conveying the concerns of political, social and business leaders.[4]

Changing workforce demographics, however, is only part of the mounting challenge. What is not well understood is that there is a second factor that will make the operational and strategic impacts of this looming brain drain potentially much more serious than business and political leaders realize. In the past 25 years, the developed world has experienced unprecedented advances in the technological and scientific domains, made possible in large part by the proliferation of information and communication technologies. Individual scientific domains, such as chemistry, physics, and genetics, along with engineering and technical fields, such as aeronautical, electrical, and network engineering, have become increasingly specialized and complex, and require a constant range and flow of high-level knowledge and technological capabilities, residing in the workforce.[5]

Furthermore, knowledge-intensive work today is more interdisciplinary than ever before, often requiring the integration of expertise across a wide range of subjects and between a greater number of individuals and organizations. In the pharmaceutical industry, for example, drug discovery today requires collaboration between experts in fields such as molecular biology, biochemistry, pharmacology, genomics, and bioinformatics. In another example, managing environmental cleanup projects requires knowledge of chemical, thermal, and fluid dynamics, along with expertise in specialized treatment processes for different pollutants, federal and state regulations, dispute resolution, and complex project management techniques.[6]

Operating in interdisciplinary and knowledge-complex environments like these, professionals and managers inevitably develop important practical knowledge about related disciplines, not to mention relationships with other experts who they can interact and exchange knowledge with. The cumulative knowledge gained by working with others in an environment that integrates such complex specialties creates types of expertise that are very hard to replicate, replace or recover. The above-mentioned threats to knowledge and wisdom of an organization are evidently very real, and now becoming immediate and urgent. Understanding the severity of the threat is a prerequisite for effective action, and consequent appropriate strategies and actions are crucial to the future performance of enterprises.

To be able to act appropriately, the concepts of knowledge and wisdom should be well understood. Knowledge is the capacity for effective action or decision-making in the context of organizational activity. It distinguishes itself from information, which is data that is structured so that it is transferable, but its immediate value depends on the user's ability to interpret and act upon it. Wisdom is knowledge combined with societal and personal values – prudence, conscientiousness, caring, etc. – concerning the impacts of actions on various stakeholders. Organizational wisdom is often seen as the virtuous habit of decisions and actions that serve the common good of the enterprise and its various stakeholders.[7]

DeLong[8] offers insightful views on 'Lost knowledge' – knowledge loss that can occur at various levels: at a broad organizational/functional level, such as the potential loss of a nuclear-testing capability; it also occurs on a work unit/small group level, as illustrated by the semi-conductor design team and on an individual level, as could happen in e.g. marketing managers 'expertise'.

DeLong also provides an appropriate typology of four distinct types of knowledge interacting in an organization at all times, which are essential to understand:[9]

- *Human Knowledge*

  This constitutes what individuals know, or know how to do. Human or individual knowledge is manifested as skill (e.g., the ability to develop a market plan, give feedback to subordinates, or program your wireless phone) or expertise (e.g., deep understanding of complex chemical reactions, the limitations of specific networking software, or the complexities of policy implementation). Human knowledge is generally described as either explicit or tacit knowledge. Human knowledge may also be sentient, that is, located in the body, such as knowing how to type or ride a bicycle. Or it may be cognitive, that is, largely conceptual and abstract.

- *Social Knowledge*

  This form of knowledge exists in relationships between individuals or within groups. It is often called "social capital". An executive with an extensive network of personal relationships with clients or a high-performing team of research scientists both reflect the presence of social knowledge embedded in those relationships. Social knowledge is largely tacit, shared by group members, and develops only as a result of working together. Its presence is reflected by high levels of trust and an ability to collaborate effectively.

- *Cultural Knowledge*

  This type of knowledge reflects a collective understanding of how activities are performed in a particular organization, that is, how to behave if you want to be accepted as a member of a particular group. While social knowledge, as previously defined, describes intellectual capital residing in specific relationships, cultural knowledge describes collective knowledge that is shared more broadly across an organization. If a top salesperson retires, he or she takes away a valuable set of relationships with clients, but the departure does not affect the cultural knowledge of the unit. If, however, most of the sales force left at once, then this collective cultural knowledge could also be affected. The loss of cultural knowledge can become particularly important in organizations experiencing very high levels of turnover.

- *Structured Knowledge*

  This type of knowledge is embedded in an organization's systems, processes, databases, tools, and routines. Knowledge in this form is explicit and rule-based. A key distinction between structured knowledge and the other types is that structured knowledge is assumed to exist independently of human 'knowers'. Thus, it is clearly an important organizational resource.

A Practical Knowledge Management (KM) Model for an Aging Workforce

The most successful organizations follow a structured, formal, and systemic approach to KM. This strategy ensures that the right questions are asked and answered in all phases of implementation. The following KM model for an aging workforce contains four phases – workforce assessment, recruitment and retention, knowledge capture and transfer, and knowledge application and measurement (Figure 6.1).[10]

Phase One – Workforce Knowledge Assessment

Preparing for the aging workforce exodus begins with workforce knowledge assessment. The planning effort should be systemic, organization-wide and aligned with the organization's strategic plan. The key steps in workforce knowledge assessment are:

- Determine the current requirements for knowledge

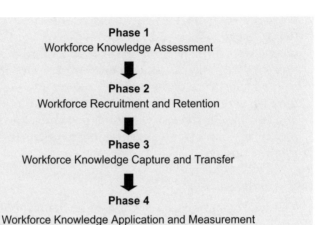

Phase 1
Workforce Knowledge Assessment

Phase 2
Workforce Recruitment and Retention

Phase 3
Workforce Knowledge Capture and Transfer

Phase 4
Workforce Knowledge Application and Measurement

Figure 6.1
A practical knowledge management model for an aging workforce

- Create a future workforce knowledge profile
- Develop the current workforce knowledge profile
- Determine knowledge gaps and surpluses
- Implement strategies to meet the knowledge gaps and reduce surpluses.

A useful approach in the first step here is to make a distinction between explicit and tacit knowledge situations and requirements. Explicit knowledge is known, documented and easily transferable knowledge, while tacit knowledge is the 'knowledge in people's heads' that is not documented and often not recognized and communicable by employees.[11] Figure 6.2 indicates the need for both types of knowledge for productivity and creativity.

Enterprise Competitive Needs

Organizational capabilities are usually the result of collective individual competencies evident throughout the organization. For example, individual competencies related to collaboration and interpersonal skills could translate into an organizational competency of 'teamwork'. Core competencies are those deeply embed-

	Productivity	Creativity
Explicit Knowledge	Efficiency Improvements (Improving Mousetrap Efficiency)	Incremental Innovation (Develop a New Mousetrap)
Tacit Knowledge	Effectiveness Improvements (New Processes Borrowed from Other Industries)	Disruptive Innovation (Develop a New Mouse-Catching Device)

Enterprise Knowledge Needs

Figure 6.2
Types of knowledge for productivity and creativity

ded capabilities that enable the enterprise to provide quality programs and services to customers. A key goal of KM must be to
preserve those capabilities within the organization as the workforce 'brain exodus' proceeds.

Identification and clear communication of organizational competencies can have a significant impact on results. In a KM context, they serve as a framework for focusing selection and development efforts that will facilitate knowledge transfer. The questions to be considered are:

- Will this position be required in the future?

- Is the particular position mission-critical to the enterprise?

- Is the position currently filled by an incumbent who has tacit
  knowledge or skills that cannot be easily replaced?

- Is the position currently filled by an incumbent who plans to
  retire in the next 12 to 24 months?

- Are particular succession or replacement strategies in place
  for identified critical workforce positions?

The first step is to identify the critical positions that meet the cri-
teria, and their occupants. Once those individual occupants of
critical positions have been identified – the 'goers' – the next step
is to analyze and document their knowledge, skills and abilities.
The documented knowledge, skills and abilities of the incum-

bents are then used as the basis for recruiting and selecting individuals – the 'comers' – who will replace the 'goers'.

Phase Two – Recruitment and Retention

The search for talent to replace those aging individuals with key knowledge involves carefully reviewing the environment in which they contribute. The first step is to determine the following:

- Who are the successful people in the position?
- What do they do that makes them successful?
- What are the hiring manager's expectations (cost, time, quality, etc.)?
- What are the metrics to measure the business impact of a great or a bad hire?

One of the key sources for finding talent is internal recruiting. Some questions to ask:

- Are there obvious candidates (i.e. someone working closely with the incumbent)?
- Can candidates be found among those positions identified as surplus?

When internal candidates are identified through this process, a development plan can be created to fill any gaps in skills and knowledge so that the 'comer' can begin the knowledge transfer process with the 'goer'. If one must look outside the company, an obvious question is if there are potential candidates among suppliers or competitors. Referrals from customers, suppliers and employees often result in candidates who come highly recommended.

Recruiting, either internally or externally, for a replacement for the aging 'goer' can be a challenging process. In order to achieve successful knowledge transfer, the organization must first have the right person identified as the 'comer'. Professional interviewing is still the most frequently used of all hiring practices. The technique that correlates most highly with quality hires is based on the foundation of competency based behavioral interviewing.

The concept behind this approach is that past performance is the best predictor of future performance. Interviewers ask for examples of specific, often critical incidents (both positive and negative outcomes) in order to draw conclusions about how a candidate would perform in the position.

Retaining critical talent within the organization in order to transfer knowledge to the potential 'comer' is one of the most cost-effective strategies used by best-practice organizations. According to numerous surveys throughout several industries, the number one reason why employees remain at an organization is the presence of good career growth and development opportunities. In the same surveys, fair pay and benefits do not rank in the top 10. Transferring critical knowledge will not only enhance the comer's career, it also will likely increase their retention.

For most organizations, the HR department can support leaders with a variety of retention policies and practices. Some questions to ask about an enterprise's capability to retain key aging employees are:

- How can the work-life balance be improved to make the organization a more attractive place to work, for longer periods of individuals' life?

- How can work assignments be made more interesting and challenging?

- To what extent are employees at all levels recognized and rewarded for their contributions?

- What career development support is available for especially older workers?

- What messages do we send to older employees to tell them they are a valued and valuable investment?

Phase Three – Knowledge Capture and Transfer

Successful enterprises develop a knowledge intensive culture by encouraging behaviors that facilitate knowledge sharing and knowledge seeking. The specific strategies an organization uses to capture and transfer knowledge should be determined by the intended outcome and the type of knowledge to be transferred, as illustrated by a company example in the following box.[12]

Knowledge Capture at SABMiller PLC

When SABMiller PLC took a close look at its staff, it realized that many of its highly skilled employees would be retiring in the not-too-distant future. In fact, the brewer projected that between 2005 and 2008 roughly 40 percent of its managers in brewery operations would reach retirement eligibility, based on their age and length of service. The reason so many Miller workers are reaching retirement at the same time? In the 1970s, the company grew substantially, building and staffing four new breweries. Many of the managers hired when the breweries opened have been there ever since. And replacing them won't be easy. These workers are considered highly skilled craftsmen, and learning how to apply the precise blend, temperature, and timing in the brewing process takes years.

To make sure that older workers don't take the bulk of the company's collective wisdom with them when they leave, Miller decided to focus on capturing the knowledge of retiring workers before they walk out the door. A three- to five-year strategic staffing initiative for its six U.S. breweries is already under way. As part of the process, Miller is undergoing a targeted staffing analysis of current jobs, forecasting future needs, and determining who has what skills.

Meanwhile, Miller is filling its talent pipeline on the other end with a college age program to recruit and train younger workers. It's important to "bring people in right out of school," says Pat Henry, Director of Strategic Projects. "They earn money while they're learning the business, and it's a perfect opportunity to transfer specialized knowledge, especially in jobs where skills are scarce."

A tack Miller is not taking is motivating its older workers to stay in the workforce longer. Henry says it's tough to sell employees on postponing their retirements. "They tend to have a date in mind, and when they're ready to go, they're ready to go," she says. But Miller encourages older folks to act as mentors, coach younger workers, or return for short-term projects or consulting assignments during peak periods. Older workers are valued for their knowledge and abilities, and "in a sense, they can't be replaced," says Henry.

But that won't stop Miller from trying. Ultimately, the brewer hopes that its recruiting, retention, and retirement efforts will result in a multigenerational workforce that is insulated from future demographic ebbs and flows.

KM practitioners have devised many creative and effective strategies to both capture and transfer knowledge critical to the organization's success. They include communities of practice (CoPs), knowledge mapping, knowledge cafes, conferences and forums, coaching/mentoring processes, best practice repositories and many others. Some of the more prominent examples are described below.

- *Document mining*

  The effective mining of existing organizational documentation for explicit and tacit knowledge, takes time but yields positive results in terms of finding mission critical and often little-known knowledge. The goal of document mining is to empower and support the knowledge worker. Document mining, which developed independently during the emergence of information technologies, is most suited for capturing knowledge that already resides within existing databases or texts. Incorporating other collaborative tools is essential to capturing the unwritten (tacit) knowledge, residing in peoples' heads.

- *Storytelling*

  The telling of enterprise and organizational stories of successes, achievements, failures and events, is an effective enabling mirror to employees. In particular, it:

  - Enables people to grasp ways of knowledgeable actions

  - Persuades people to change

  - Facilitates people to work together

  - Assists in sharing knowledge (critical to the enterprise)

  - Removes false images and impressions

  - Communicates the requirements of positions and occupants

  - Transmits values, both personal and organizational

  - Leads people into a knowledgeable risk-taking future

- *Knowledge mapping*

  A knowledge map is an active, visual representation of the firm's intellectual capital. Generally deployed on the Intranet or Internet, the knowledge map is the means to design or set out a business or enterprise body of knowledge, and then to be format-ready to communicate it to its people. It provides a visual display of:

  - The enterprise format (business model) and its structures (organizational architecture)

  - People's roles and responsibilities, and network of interactions

  - The business processes and the associated knowledge people will need in carrying out their day-to-day jobs

  - Access to the knowledge needed to perform both explicit and tacit knowledge

  - Experts in the firm and how to contact them

  The goals of knowledge mapping efforts should be made clear to all employees from the outset, as well as regularly, to guide the enterprise toward both efficiency and effectiveness. The best way is to set out how work (as they link to core processes) is performed for development, effectiveness, training, reference, business improvement or broad deployment to new employees.

- *Communities of Practice (COPs)*

  CoPs are now validated as one of the most successful techniques a firm can install as part of its KM system. It involves the purposeful and cohered enabling of a group of people, across organizations, enterprises and even functions, to relate to each other based on mutual interests and practices. COPs assist enterprises in learning – gaining new knowledge – from a broad array of people, both inside and outside the enterprise. Many pioneering enterprises in KM have CoPs. According to findings from the American Productivity & Quality Center (APQC), a best practice example is Halliburton, which now has 17,000 collaboration hits with 3,100 unique users per month involved in their community COP project.

There are a number of strategies used by enterprises to ensure effective knowledge application. The truly successful application strategies are a mix of tactics that support knowledge transfer, and involve both the 'comer' and the 'goer' with learning that leaves an enduring legacy. This approach creates a culture that values and rewards learning, a prerequisite for any effective KM initiative. Below is a diverse sample list of best-practice strategies from several well-known business publications or conferences, and the enterprises that have successfully applied them:

- KM repository/library database (Atlas Electronics; Meyer Werft, Siemens)
- Employee best practice identification process (Wells Fargo)
- Annual KM summit/symposium (Intel)
- Floating coach (Charles Schwab)
- CoP (The World Bank; Siemens)
- Formal transfer process using knowledge experts as facilitators (Shell Oil)
- Enterprise portal (Air Products and Chemicals).

One of the major lagging competencies in KM has been measuring its effects in the enterprise. After establishing baseline performance levels to measure the impact of the KM method or strategy, it is important to link the results to the performance of the business process, product or service outcomes, or other business operations that are being energized by increased KM capabilities. Measurement is the area of KM most important to the enterprise's 'bottom line' of profitability.

Carter identifies four conditions that can impede or destroy the implementation of a KM model for an aging workforce.[13] They are:

- *Lack of an enterprise sponsor*

  The absence of an executive 'champion' to support the KM initiative is a set-up for failure – it is essential for KM success.

- *Lack of a pilot program*

  Little learning and course correction can occur if enterprises do not "start small" and use a pilot program for learning.

- *Lack of a clear strategy*

  The KM initiative needs to be grounded in a clear strategic goal with approaches that will produce desired results.

- *Picking the wrong place or the wrong problem*

  This can be especially damaging to ultimate success. Choices made early on, during the pilot phase, are extremely important.

A useful enterprise application of knowledge sharing is illustrated by Voelpel & Han (Table 6.1).[14]

Table 6.1

An overview of the motivations for, barriers to and managerial implications of knowledge sharing in Siemens Sharenet

Motivations *for using Siemens ShareNet*	*From the knowledge contributor's viewpoint:* • Incentives (monetary and non-monetary) • Cultural motivation such as collectivism, Confucian Dynamism (in the Chinese context) • Demonstrate their presence and expertise via ShareNet *From the knowledge receiver's viewpoint:* • Time saving and productivity enhancement • Access to approved solutions and answers to problems • Finding capable people who can provide help based on their experiences
Barriers *to using Siemens ShareNet (in the Chinese context)*	• Language barriers • Cultural barriers (face saving, in-group/out-group distinction) • Unreliability of the incentive system • Operative barriers (complexity of the system and structure) • Miscellaneous barriers (e.g. lack of time)
Managerial Implications: *How to overcome barriers and* **increase knowledge-sharing**	• Introduce a Chinese language sub area for knowledge sharing • Building long-term staff loyalty and a strong company culture • 'Career involvement' as a powerful incentive for participation • Top management support • Enabling cross-business division knowledge sharing • Stable ('symbolic'-based) incentive system • Lower entry barriers to usage

How to Retain Critical Knowledge: A Knowledge-Retention Framework and Actions

Because of the dangers of 'lost knowledge' due to the aging workforce, knowledge retention becomes extremely important as part of the above-mentioned KM model and deserves particular attention. Figure 6.3 illustrates a knowledge-retention framework.[15]

The six key dimensions of the above-mentioned knowledge-retention framework are each briefly highlighted below.

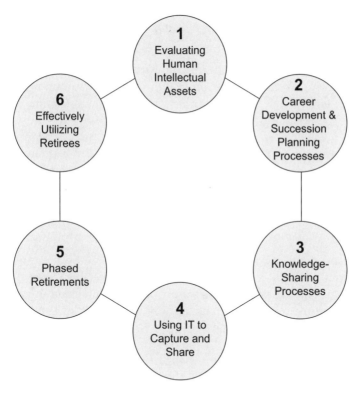

Figure 6.3
*Knowledge-retention framework for an aging workforce,
with six key dimensions*

- *Evaluating Human Intellectual Assets*

One of the first steps in diagnosing where an organization is most at risk of losing knowledge, is having a detailed process to track current skill inventories and future needs for all essential professional and management roles in the organization. This enables extensive succession planning for professional as well as managerial positions. Most importantly, it helps the organization to identify future knowledge gaps that are likely to emerge, given retirement eligibility and historical retirement patterns. This allows more effective resource allocation around knowledge retention initiatives.

- *Career Development/Succession Planning Processes*

An important element for retaining employees and building long-term workforce capabilities is the existence of extensive career development and succession planning processes to complement an enterprise's skills inventory system. While a skills management process monitors the current and future state of resources needed, a career development program assists in building the knowledge and competencies professionals and managers need to prepare for future roles. Succession planning and career paths show employees the opportunities that are available or emerging.

- *Knowledge-Sharing Practices*

To address problems of knowledge retention created by an aging workforce, companies have to institutionalize an elaborate set of knowledge-sharing practices that must become embedded in enterprise culture, and accepted as the way work is done. The first step in developing these practices is to inventory and evaluate those that the organization already has in place. An integral part of the techniques used for knowledge transfer will also be the cultural values and norms needed to support knowledge-sharing behaviors.

- *Using Information Technology to Capture and Share Knowledge*

IT resources form an important part of any knowledge retention strategy, but executives must be careful not to view technology as the solution to their knowledge retention problems. IT applications are only enablers – they cannot meet knowledge transfer objectives on their own. To retain knowledge for the organization, line managers must make sure that IT applications are part of a comprehensive effort that also changes practices, processes, and behaviors. The technology applications that can support knowledge retention objectives include:

- Databases to track skills and competencies: For example, Shell Chemical is building a talent management database to help identify current and emerging gaps, as well as future technical skill needs.

- Lessons-learned repositories: This is a solution that holds promise in some settings, but such databases also require considerable behavioral change to make sure they are kept up-to-date and actually used.

- Communication and knowledge-sharing systems: These applications support distributed organizations or virtual communities of practice. Buckman Laboratories has been among the most successful at building a global knowledge-sharing infrastructure with its K'Netix system, which combines electronic bulletin boards, virtual conference rooms, libraries, and email. Buckman's investment has also been supported by a major culture change to encourage use of the technology.

- Systems to support diagnostic and problem solving behaviors: Consumers should pilot software that leads users through a highly structured diagnostic process to solve production problems and capture the solutions. Combined with a culture change initiative, this application helps surface the tacit knowledge of veteran operators and transfers it into the system for future use.

- Automation of more routine information processing tasks – companies could introduce a web-based tool that can collect data from plant personnel describing a production problem to consulting engineers. Prompting plant workers through a diagnostic process helps them learn how to think about future problems, and over time provides a broader set of embedded solutions to consider, freeing engineers to work on the most difficult problems.

- E-learning applications – companies can capture expert knowledge into computer-based learning methodologies before a particular specialist retires. These web-based applications are still relatively new.

The following example (see box) illustrates how a company uses a database to capture knowledge.[16]

How Bosch Preserves Critical Knowledge Before It Walks out the Door

Bosch, a German provider of automotive, industrial and consumer products, introduced an interesting method for retaining critical knowledge in the organization. Older workers who possess critical knowledge and are about to retire are asked to take part in a special program. Prior to retirement, these employees fill in a form about the knowledge they gained during their careers. This information is synthesized and captured in a database used by project managers around the world. If these project managers have a difficult project that requires specialist knowledge, they can search the database to determine if there are retired workers that fit their needs. These people are then asked to work for a short period of time during the project and support the team by bringing in knowledge gained during their previous tenure with the company.

- *Phased Retirements*

Early retirements have been standard practice in many industries, but as knowledge retention and recruiting problems become more acute, companies may begin to look for ways to extend the tenure of their most valuable employees. The most common practice is known as "flexible phased retirement", which means allowing older employees to create more varied and shorter work schedules. Unfortunately, a range of legal barriers restricting pension payments still makes it difficult for private sector companies to implement formal phased retirement programs in many countries. Knowledgeable observers, however, expect these laws to be eased in the near future.

The problem of keeping older, experienced managers and professionals on the job is especially complicated for global firms, which must contend with a variety of mandatory retirement laws that are continually changing. For example, mandatory retirement in the Netherlands recently dropped from 65 to 62, creating major succession planning headaches for companies operating there. In Japan, meanwhile, the current mandatory retirement age is 60, but executives are expecting it to be raised to 65 to help ease the country's labor shortage. These changes add additional complexity to the challenges of knowledge transfer and succession planning.

- *Programs to Effectively Utilize Retirees*

The easiest knowledge retention tactic to employ when threatened with the possible loss of expertise, is hiring recent retirees back as contractors or consultants. Retirees not only have the skills needed, but they also know the culture and organizational history and have the extensive social networks necessary to get their jobs done, even when these jobs are different from those they had before. Using retirees as contractors is a double-edged sword – it helps retain access to irreplaceable expertise, but it can also create a false sense of security that the organization still controls that knowledge. *More importantly, when older workers are routinely hired back as contractors they have much less incentive to share their knowledge with others before retiring.*

Barriers to Organizational Knowledge Retention

DeLong identifies five barriers to organizational knowledge retention, which have to be well understood if a knowledge-retention framework and actions should be successfully implemented:[17]

- The cost of lost knowledge is largely hidden: For example, what is the cost of delaying the introduction of a new product that was being worked on by a recently retired scientist? And what is the cost of reduced efficiency or increased errors in a plant where two first-line supervisors just retired? Answering questions like these can provide a starting point for investigations and to provide solutions when faced with such realities.

- Uncertainty about where the firm is most vulnerable to lost knowledge: Often managers cannot get support for pursuing knowledge retention efforts because no one is clear where the greatest risks are for the company. A more strategic approach to workforce planning can help a firm identify these risks and see where it is most vulnerable to the loss of specialized expertise.

- No clear ownership of the problem: Knowledge managers are interested but often seem preoccupied with other initiatives, whereas IT managers believe they own the capability and enabling technology to drive knowledge capture. While HR owns the processes for recruiting and retaining people, it is functional and line managers who must create the values and culture that support behaviors needed to share, capture, and apply tacit knowledge derived from experience. In practice, improving knowledge retention then must be a line management concern because that's where the challenges of transferring knowledge are best understood.

- Too busy for knowledge-sharing activities: A major problem is that companies often cannot afford large-scale knowledge-sharing activities due to limitations in time, money, and people flexibility. Even when the problem of knowledge transfer is recognized, the resources needed to allow younger employees to learn from older ones are virtually gone. One challenge for cost-driven companies is to figure out how to improve knowledge transfer in an environment where interactions between retiring professionals and managers and their replacements are limited.

- Capturing knowledge is inadequate on its own: Finally, transferring knowledge within an organization is useless unless those acquiring it have the ability to learn from others and make improved decisions. Younger employees often lack the problem solving skills – and sense of empowerment – to make decisions based on knowledge passed on by more experienced employees. Companies concerned about knowledge retention also need to evaluate the quality of the problem solving skills their younger employees have.

How to Transfer Tacit Knowledge, Wisdom and "Deep Smarts" of an Aging Workforce

Building on their earlier works on knowledge assets as well as an extensive empirical study, Leonard and Swap proposed the concept of 'deep smarts' and analyzed and discussed the issue of how to cultivate and transfer this enduring business wisdom, rooted in experience and insight.[18] They term deep smarts as the "knowledge that provides a distinctive advantage, both for organizations and for managers as individuals."

Deep smarts are experience-based and as such cannot be produced overnight or imported readily. The complete definition reads: "Deep smarts are a potent form of expertise based on first-hand life experiences, providing insights drawn from tacit knowledge, and shaped by beliefs and social forces. Deep smarts are as close as we get to wisdom. They are based on know-how more than know-what – the ability to comprehend complex, interactive relationships and make swift, expert decisions based on that system level comprehension but also the ability, when necessary, to dive into component parts of that system and understand the details. Deep smarts cannot be attained through formal education alone – but they can be deliberately nourished and grown and, with dedication, transferred or recreated."

Leonard and Swap contend that the "most valuable part of deep smarts is the tacit know-how (and often, know-who) that a person has built up over years of experience." That is what makes deep smarts so difficult to transfer. In fact, they conclude that the central paradox in transferring deep smarts is that constantly reinventing the wheel is inefficient, but people learn only by doing. Finally, Leonard and Swap propose four ways of actively transferring and recreating deep smarts by guided experience: guided practice, guided observation, guided problem solving, and guided experimentation. These involve, among others, mentoring and coaching activities as well as showing and feedback sessions in order to foster and recreate deep smarts, which are based largely on pattern recognition, and are highly contextual.

The concept of deep smarts, in a way, is similar to that of "phronesis" since both, in essence, mean practical wisdom.[19] However, deep smarts are foremost about business wisdom, while phronesis is a much wider concept. Besides, in contrast to deep smarts, "phronesis" is not only about knowledge and wisdom but also includes a moral dimension and aspects of aesthetics. That might be also one of the reasons why Leonard and Swap posit that deep smarts "are not 'wisdom' in that sense – but they're as close to wisdom as business gets."

According to DeLong's framework, there are – at least – the following practices for implicit and tacit knowledge transfer: after-action reviews, mentoring programs, communities of practice, and storytelling.[20] These practices have been widely treated in the extant literature.

- *Storytelling*

  This practice has briefly been mentioned before, and deserves further elaboration in this section. Storytelling is the way people make meaning out of their experiences: people share knowledge, understanding and meaning everyday through the stories that they tell. Stories reveal what employees think about their leaders, colleagues, competitors, suppliers and customers. The following box illustrates how one organization uses storytelling to transfer knowledge.[21]

How The World Bank Uses Storytelling to Capture and Transfer Knowledge

To retain valuable experiences, share lessons learned, expand the organization's knowledge base and improve operational and product quality, The World Bank captures videos and audiotapes of selected individuals and groups involved in challenging projects. Using storytelling techniques, the Bank seeks to uncover new knowledge from the practitioners in developing countries. Interviewees are encouraged to focus on telling stories, rather than providing general observations, so the material will be more interesting for the intended audiences. This knowledge retention initiative uses subject matter experts to conduct interviews, as well as to screen and edit the videos and audiotapes, pushing relevant insights and content to audiences through a variety of media.

In coordination with its well-conceived elicitation technique, The World Bank's knowledge dissemination process also contributes

---

to its success. Both audio and videotaped interviews are posted to a Web site and burned onto CD-ROMs, with any documents referred to during the interview appearing as hot links in the final text. The World Bank also pushes these debriefings to a distribution list of targeted members, rather than simply passively posting them on the Internet. For reinforcement, they also make interviewees available for follow-up and mentoring.

Since storytelling is a natural societal behavior, the major question is whether it is used to support or undermine knowledge retention. From this perspective, it is important to understand that one of the major values of stories is their ability to communicate knowledge that cannot be represented as explicit propositions or rules. Stories can be effective for transferring both implicit knowledge about how things get done as well as deeper tacit knowledge that reflects the values that are shaping behaviors.

For example, the senior hotel designer for a large entertainment company has more than 40 years of experience building hotels. When less experienced members of the design team seek his advice, he often responds by telling stories describing previous designs that succeeded or failed. When trying to decide what size guest rooms should be in a new hotel, the veteran designer tells stories from his past experiences that show larger rooms produce more satisfied return guests, even though smaller rooms are more cost-effective to build. These stories not only help young designers understand all the factors that go into decisions about room size but they also communicate a value that holds long-term customer satisfaction as being more important than short-term cost considerations.

While stories are inherently recognized as valuable by many employees, the idea of intentionally pursuing them as a knowledge transfer tactic is sometimes regarded with suspicion or doubt, because stories violate Western business norms that value analysis over narrative. In reality, stories are a critical building block for the transfer – and retention – of the most critical and valuable knowledge in organizations.

Guidelines to use storytelling are:

a) Be clear about the purpose of using stories.

b) Create regular occasions for telling stories.

c) Ensure that the audience has adequate context to be able to interpret the lessons in experts' stories.

d) With stories that are not told face-to-face, be careful to evaluate their 'packaging' and presentation, and how narratives should be validated.

- *Mentoring and coaching*

Mentoring and coaching are among the most effective ways of directly transferring critical implicit and tacit work-related knowledge from one individual to another. Mentoring supports the sharing of the broadest range of knowledge, from detailed technical skills and tacit cultural values to career development advice, in a relationship that ideally allows the expert to monitor the degree to which knowledge is actually being absorbed. The following box provides an example of how an organization uses a mentoring program to capture, share and transfer knowledge.[22]

NASA's Mentoring Program: 'Leaders as Teachers and Mentors'

Several U.S. government agencies have begun to take proactive steps to stem the hemorrhage of knowledge. For example, the emeritus program at the NASA Goddard Space Flight Center allows retired employees to continue as valued contributors to activities and volunteer their services. Goddard's recently retired chief information officer was involved in the emeritus program and shared his wealth of knowledge, and invaluable experiences with others.

In another example, through its Academy of Program and Project Leadership's (APPL) Knowledge Sharing Initiative, NASA conducts knowledge sharing workshops, master project managers forums, and other workshops to capture, share, and transfer project management knowledge from experienced project managers (both senior level and retiree) to up-and-coming project leaders. Their "Leaders as Teachers and Mentors" program has an expert database of current and retired practitioners who make themselves available for consultation.

Depending on the context, mentoring (or coaching) can help transfer technical, operational, or managerial skills, i.e. how to perform specific aspects of a job. Mentoring also helps a newcomer learn who, how, when and why things are done in the organization. Providing orientation and introductions to influential decision makers and specialized experts helps less experienced employees develop the relationships they will need to succeed in the organization.

Mentors can also pass on cultural knowledge about organizational values and norms of behavior. Because this knowledge is tacit, it is almost always communicated by observing the mentor as a role model or symbol of effective performance. There are significant barriers to implementing successful mentoring programs, which should be recognized and managed – such as interpersonal rivalries and cultural impediments.

Guidelines to use mentoring and coaching successfully are:

a) Focus efforts on critical areas.

b) Anticipate time and resource constraints.

c) Train mentors specifically on how they can help their protégés.

d) Create an effective infrastructure to support mentoring.

e) Recognize and manage the barriers to mentoring programs.

- *After-action reviews (AARs)*

In the process of working in today's complex, high-pressure environments, a great deal of potential learning is wasted because employees often have no process to reflect on their actions, capture this new knowledge, and integrate it back into ongoing activities. An increasing number of organizations are using after-action reviews (AARs) to generate, retain, and reuse knowledge that is a by-product of ongoing operations. An AAR is a brief, focused process that helps groups to crystallize and validate new knowledge or learning from a recent event or project that all members have participated in, and is an ideal practice to capture and transfer the knowledge of an aging workforce. The process is built around five questions:

(1) What is supposed to happen?

(2) What actually happened?

(3) Why have there been deviations?

(4) What can we learn from this and do differently next time?

(5) How should we capture this knowledge and use it for future organizational learning?

AARs are flexible processes that can also be used to help groups identify what they need to learn in order to improve performance. In these processes, the objective is to improve the dynamics of knowledge transfer between veterans and less experienced employees, in part because it applies expertise directly to current or future problems.

While storytelling and mentoring are practices that can transfer existing knowledge that will otherwise be lost, today's volatile work environment demands new knowledge to be constantly created to respond effectively. This means when teams are not proactively learning from their experiences, they are actually losing knowledge that could be valuable to the organization. AARs help create this new knowledge in a team setting that also increases the opportunities for its retention.

- *Communities of Practice (CoPs)*

  As previously mentioned, CoPs have generated a lot of interest in recent years, as organizations recognize the value of supporting natural interest groups that share common languages, values, and problems. These natural communities – or networks – can be leveraged to improve knowledge sharing and problem solving across organizational boundaries, and they have proved their value in doing so. CoPs have an additional benefit when lost knowledge is a concern for management – supporting the connections and health of communities of key types of experts or managers can go a long way to enabling the retention of both critical individuals and their knowledge in the organization.

Communities of practice can provide particular organizational benefits in several ways. A well-organized CoP can enable professionals who feel isolated with a much-needed sense of connectedness to others inside and outside the organization, who are facing similar challenges and who have similar perspectives on key capability practices and their organizational value-added. CoPs encourage employees to share their expertise more broadly, thus making this knowledge more likely to survive in the organization after a single expert leaves.

Communities of practice also provide resources for bringing new members of the community along the learning curve more quickly than through traditional methods only. They do this partly by making available the latest codified knowledge in a particular domain – for example, FAQs on a website – or by speeding up the development of a new member's social capital through joining an active network of experts oriented toward sharing with and supporting each other.

In reality, there are many types of communities or networks that can improve organizational knowledge retention if they are supported effectively. Saint-Onge and Wallace identify five characteristics that define successful communities:[23]

1. *Conversations*: Productive questions and discussions are the key to learning. In effective communities, all members are encouraged to express opinions, discuss problems, and promote their successors.

2. *Collaboration*: Learning usually happens through social interaction. Successful CoPs support mutual problem solving and knowledge sharing among colleagues in non-hierarchical exchanges.

3. *Commitment*: Effective communities consist of members who believe it is important to contribute their time to support the group's purpose. They believe in the value of their community, and senior management display commitment to the importance of communities for knowledge transfer and retention by making adequate resources available to help build and sustain them.

4. *Connectivity*: Communities are only valuable when their members have ways of easily connecting, whether it is face-to-face in periodic forums or conferences, or by using an elaborate technology infrastructure that supports electronic communication and collaboration tools.

5. *Capabilities*: Finally, effective communities continually build, refresh, and sustain the skills, attitudes, values, and knowledge that organizations need to implement their strategic objectives.

In an increasingly aging workforce environment, the above-mentioned four practices of storytelling, mentoring & coaching, after-action reviews, and COPs in transferring knowledge assume crucial importance. The measure of successful implementation of such practices will be the differentiating factor between sustainable enterprises and those that become less innovative through loss of crucial knowledge.

Knowledge-Recovery Initiatives

In view of current demographic trends, there is going to be a much greater loss of vital knowledge in organizations that have become more technologically and structurally complex in the past decade. In most of the 20th century, a tremendous amount of knowledge was always leaving organizations, but it did not matter because it was relatively obsolete or could be easily replaced. Now, in the knowledge-networked innovation economy and aging society, it is a different matter.

Managers can use three strategies to recover critical intellectual capital when employees have left the organization: engaging retirees; outsourcing intellectual activities; and regeneration of knowledge.[24] A prerequisite for these strategies (discussed below) is particularly concerning employees that could depart with hard-to-replace knowledge essential to future effectiveness. Leaders want to keep the experiential knowledge of former employees (e.g., know-how, know-who, know-where) accessible to the organization for use in ongoing operations or special projects, to solve unexpected problems, or to pass on to successors.

The solution here means keeping former employees connected to the organization by rehiring them as contractors or consultants. But when rehiring ex-employees is not a viable solution, then the management must decide between outsourcing as a way of replacing diminished competencies or regenerating these capabilities inside the organization.

Three strategies to recover enterprise-critical knowledge are:

- *Engaging retirees*

  Enterprises can use several different approaches to engaging retirees:

  (1) Some have strict policies against rehiring them.

  (2) Many more bring retirees back as contractors or consultants only by informal arrangements with individual managers.

  (3) Some have tried to limit the practice of rehiring by implementing policies that dictate in what situations retirees can be brought back into their organizations.

  (4) A few enterprises, such as Monsanto, MITRE, and Cigna Insurance, have created formal programs to actually encourage the reemployment of retirees.

  (5) A network of retirees in the industry – from various enterprise backgrounds – can be created and stimulated to recreate the required knowledge.

Given the looming shortage of experienced professional and managerial talent in certain industries and professions, it is only a matter of time until more enterprises will have to shift to an approach of engaging retirees. When it comes to utilizing ex-employees, whether they are retired or at mid-career, every organization's situation will be somewhat different. Leveraging effectively the critical knowledge and skills of former employees involves knowing the enterprise options, and the advantages and disadvantages of each. Enterprises are well advised to:

  a) Create a formal program to manage a pool of skilled retirees available for temporary assignments.

b) Proactively track the expertise and availability of former employees for consulting assignments.

c) Encourage managers to routinely seek ways to stay connected with former employees.

d) Create the infrastructure to support an alumni community.

e) Cast the network wider than only own retirees, into the larger arena of retirees in the industry.

f) Let contracting and consulting agreements with ex-employees remain an informal process handled by individual managers.

The last method is the way most organizations deal with retirees today. Contracting agreements are based primarily on personal relationships between managers and retirees. This may seem like the most practical approach, but it can also undermine knowledge transfer practices among older employees who know their expertise is the platform for a possible comfortable consulting relationship after they retire.

- *Outsourcing intellectual activities*

  Most outsourcing decisions have historically been a matter of management choice, and outsourcing is well-known in non-intellectual, low-cost environments. Leaders outsource single tasks, functions, or entire processes to cut costs or because they believe there is strategic advantage in reallocating their in-house resources. It is a completely different matter if there is no choice, when experts whose knowledge underlies a specific capability may be retiring, and it is impossible or unrealistic to replace them to maintain the same level of performance. It is quite feasible that some retirees cannot work the required hours as contractors, or they can't fill the same roles they left, or management can't risk critical operations on part-timers. In such cases, the outsourcing of intellectual activities may no longer be optional.

  There are 5 principles to keep in mind before entering into an outsourcing contract as a way of recovering knowledge:

  a) Organizational strategy should drive outsourcing decisions.

b) Employee turnover puts different types of knowledge at risk, and this should be well recognized.

c) The risks of outsourcing specific knowledge must be evaluated.

d) The stability of an outsourced supplier's base must be evaluated.

e) A top management sponsor (champion) for key knowledge outsourcing is essential.

- *Regeneration of knowledge*

Critical knowledge can disappear overnight from an enterprise. It is a crisis if that knowledge cannot be outsourced and the former source of knowledge is not available for consulting. Executives rarely think about strategies and tactics for re-creating lost knowledge, and although there is no easy approach and methodology for solving this problem, there are five major guidelines for action when it happens:

(1) In the area where departing experts have left a gap, determine what knowledge their successors actually possess.

(2) Use existing artifacts and documentation, even if limited, to spark ideas and questions.

(3) Reconstruct the relevant professional and social network of veteran employees who have departed.

(4) Hire an outside consultant who is an expert in the area where knowledge has been lost.

(5) Re-create knowledge by focusing on specific problems related to a position, and not just in general linked to a position's overall responsibilities.

It is an inescapable fact that many enterprises in especially the developed world are going to lose more and more critical intellectual capital in the immediate years and decades ahead. In some cases, this is going to have a serious impact on enterprise performance. Leaders who want to minimize the damage caused by lost knowledge must seriously consider the strategies their organizations will use to deal with essential intellectual capital once it is gone. In some cases, executives will retain access to knowledge by rehiring retirees. In other instances, outsourcing will make the most relevant option. Sometimes there will be no choice but to look for ways to regenerate certain knowledge the particular enterprise area, position or function once had, by focusing on specific problems and their solutions. Understanding these options is a prerequisite to making the best decisions in each situation.

KM and Overall Enterprise Sustainability: The Systemic Context of the Aging Workforce

We are increasingly living in a world of linked systems, with globally-linked demand and supply value chains becoming more and more prevalent. Management of an enterprise does not only have to consider the management of knowledge inside its own enterprise but also in its linked partners in supply and demand chains. As previously mentioned, the theory of constraints (TOC) specifies that a dynamic system is only as good as its weakest link. *Effective knowledge management concerning an aging workforce is a network-wide, corporate-wide, operating unit, functional and group-wide issue.* No matter where future knowledge resources are seen as a potential threat to the enterprise, thinking strategically (including systemically) about the solution will determine the future sustainability and performance of the enterprise.

Four major guidelines must be considered:[25]

- *Linking knowledge management to the enterprise's strategy*

  In the process of exploring risks posed by lost knowledge, different business strategies will create more vulnerability in certain enterprise activities. Firms placing a priority on innovation capabilities will probably want to look first at R&D processes, while those pursuing a growth strategy might be more concerned with production and sales.

  A low-cost enterprise strategy puts an emphasis on sustaining production and maintenance capabilities within tight cost parameters. When evaluating capabilities relative to competitors – an emphasis on enterprise differentiation strategy – retaining unique knowledge in e.g. R&D, marketing, sales, and delivery processes are of most concern. One common characteristic of lost knowledge is that, when not taking a strategic perspective, management can easily overlook threats that could undermine core operational processes.

- *Taking a systemic perspective with knowledge management being one of four enterprise views*

Lost knowledge always represents a complex problem that cannot be solved by isolating it from the organizational system that produced the lost knowledge – and this system can only be understood in the context within which it is embedded. Managers need to examine the situation from at least four perspectives, as illustrated in Figure 6.4.

In Figure 6.4, the *operational perspective* is held by those closest to the activity where the knowledge is applied in the enterprise. It indicates specifically what essential enterprise systems the particular knowledge affects. For example, the marketing

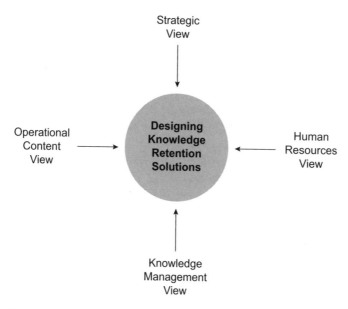

Figure 6.4
An enterprise systemic perspective of knowledge management

manager's knowledge of customers affects decision-making about where, when, and how to market a product, which directly influences sales.

The *strategic view* locates the knowledge in a larger organizational context. One may find that such marketing managers are working on products that are strategically important to the company, or they may be relatively unimportant to future objectives. Consequently, this perspective, mainly held by senior executives, determines whether the potential lost knowledge has implications for the firm's ability to implement its strategy.

The *HR perspective* considers the larger environment in which the knowledge holder operates. It explores how knowledge holders are recruited, developed, why they leave, and how their replacements are recruited. The HR view provides a contextual or larger systems perspective on the environment that has shaped the knowledge holders. Questions are addressed such as: How are marketing managers recruited? What are their official and actual career paths? What does the culture do to encourage employee turnover? How does compensation affect knowledge sharing?

- *Viewing existing knowledge as a resource for learning from the external environment*

  Simply thinking of intellectual capital as an asset to be protected is a dangerously narrow approach because it can overlook important impacts of lost knowledge. A strategic perspective must also consider how knowledge affects an organization's capacity for learning and change. Losing extensive experiential knowledge related to strategically important activities degrades the enterprise's ability to learn from the external environment. Experiential knowledge is a key component in interpreting inputs from the environment and helping the organization to respond effectively.

- *Taking a long-term perspective on the problems of lost knowledge*

  While short-term threats of knowledge loss will increasingly affect enterprises, a strategic perspective means viewing knowledge management as a long-term effort. This must become an embedded way of thinking for management if organizations are to sustain workforce capabilities in the face of shifting demographics and looming shortages of skilled workers.

A key premise already indicated above is that any knowledge management strategy should fit into the organization's strategic management approach. Large bureaucratic organizations that pursue a "rationally deliberate" strategic planning process are going to be comfortable with a more formalized approach to planning for knowledge retention. On the other hand, smaller, more dynamic organizations that use an "adaptively emergent" strategic planning process will be better served by an approach that supports a more flexible portfolio of projects. Part of the long-term perspective is also recognizing that enterprise thinking about knowledge management solutions will evolve, and therefore not remain static or amenable to fixed solutions.

Key Pointers of Chapter 6

- Knowledge-loss threats to enterprises due to the aging workforce are serious and immediate. The impact of the expected "brain exodus" is one problem, but combined with that are the unprecedented advances in technology and scientific domains. The concepts of organizational knowledge and wisdom should be well understood and managed.

- A practical knowledge management model for an aging workforce consists of four phases: workforce knowledge assessment; workforce recruitment and retention; knowledge capture and transfer; and knowledge application and measurement. Four preconditions for successful implementation of a KM model were outlined.

- Critical enterprise knowledge can be retained through a knowledge-retention framework for an aging workforce, consisting of six important elements (or steps): evaluating human intellectual assets; career development/succession planning processes; knowledge sharing practices; using IT to capture and share knowledge; phased retirements; and programs to effectively utilize retirees. Several barriers to organizational knowledge retention exist, and these should be well understood and overcome.

- Practices for transferring implicit & tacit knowledge, and wisdom & "deep smarts", include storytelling, after-action reviews, mentoring programs, and communities of practice.

- Knowledge-recovering initiates to include the engagement of retirees, outsourcing of intellectual activities, and regeneration of knowledge.

- Knowledge management of an aging workforce should not be viewed in isolation, but regarded systemically in context of the overall enterprise strategy.

7 The Third V-Field: Health Management Approaches for the Aging Workforce

Key Issues of this Chapter

- Health is more than just a physical issue in an aging workforce
- Fitness is not a matter of age
- Mental health management of an aging workforce
- Physical health management of an aging workforce
- Emotional health management of an aging workforce
- Integrated health management tools to increase productivity and creativity of an aging workforce

Health is More than Just a Physical Issue for an Aging Workforce

Most jobs do not require workers to perform at their top physical capacity. In a knowledge-intensive world, most new value-added to companies arises from mental work – talent and skills application – and not physical work. And both mental and physical work are affected by the emotional state of the individual and his/her organizational or community group – emotions of confidence, happiness, belonging, patience/frustration, esteem (self-esteem and group esteem), fear, motivation, and other feelings.

The three concepts of mental, physical and emotional health are of course closely linked. For example, some observers view emotional health as a state of mind, which is largely related to physical well-being. So it is difficult to separate these issues – it is done here in this chapter for discussion only, but it is essential to view workforce health as an integrated concept. The last section of this chapter presents a tool for such an essentially integrated view.

An important reason for viewing aging workforce health as more than just a physical issue is the changing requirements for enterprise competitiveness in a knowledge-networked innovation economy. Creative inputs for innovative value-added to enterprises are becoming more crucial than physical, repetitive inputs. This requires mental and emotional human capabilities of a high and consistent nature. With the dramatic shift towards an aging workforce, an expanded and integrated view of worker health is therefore crucial to future sustainability and performance of an enterprise.

One such integrated view is the concept of 'workability', developed by the Finnish Institute of Occupational Health.[1] Workability means the sum of factors relating to both the individual's overall health and functional capacities, and the work/value-added requirements that are important for the future performance of the enterprise. In other words, workability is the product of the interaction between work and the resources of the individual – physical, mental and emotional. The concept of workability – and a Workability Index – is further elaborated in the last section of this chapter.

To examine the relationship between aging and performance, some researchers, especially Heike Bruch and her team at University of St. Gallen in Switzerland, use the framework of organizational energy.[2] Organizational energy is defined as the force a company purposefully works with – it reflects the extent to which an organization has mobilized its emotional, mental and physical energy potential relating to an aging workforce, in pursuit of its goals.

For the first time in history, the powerful role that emotions play in shaping corporate energy and behavior is being intensively explored. In essence, the task of 'unleashing' organizational energy by capturing workers' emotional excitement, engagement of their mental capacities, and producing physical well-being for taking action is now recognized. With its close link to emotional health of an aging workforce, the concept of organizational energy is further discussed later in this chapter (see 'Emotional Health Management of an Aging Workforce').

Fitness is Not a Matter of Age

Considerable misunderstandings about the concepts of age and fitness exist. Age is not a disease – it is a biological process of change that starts at birth. The aging process means that people may not have the same strength or physical abilities at 60 or 70 that they had at 25 or 30. But in the case of most jobs, with minor adaptations or adjustments, workers can perform the required work very well into their 70s and sometimes beyond. *In some types of work, performance may continue to improve into the 60s and 70s.*

Age certainly does not determine fitness levels – studies show that with regular physical exercise, physical capacity can remain relatively unchanged between ages 45 to 65. It also means that 45-year-old workers who do not exercise can be less fit than co-workers aged 65 or older who do look after their health.[3]

However, as people grow older, everyone is affected by physical conditions and fitness levels in some way or another. Physical and cognitive abilities slowly diminish as part of the natural aging process. Vision, hearing, and balance decline gradually with age. But as health and longevity improve, the timing and pace of these physical changes are delayed.

In some occupations, older employees may work less swiftly, struggle with physically strenuous tasks, learn unfamiliar material more slowly, and have more difficulty juggling many tasks at once. *However, contrary to popular misconceptions, workers over age 55 do not, in general, sustain more injuries or absences than their younger counterparts.*[4] But when they are ill or injured, their recovery times are longer. Of course, older workers have higher incidences of degenerative conditions such as arthritis and age-related illnesses such as hypertension and heart disease, and so their health-care costs on average rise with age. But employers can adjust the physical environment – e.g., better lighting and acoustics (see Chapter 8) – offer regular health screening, and encourage or provide fitness programs.

A key question is: do any of the above-mentioned diminished abilities lead to low levels of productivity and creativity? With their extensive knowledge and experience, older workers can compensate, often by better focusing on essential decisions or actions – they work smarter due to their greater experience. An AARP study asked employers to rank the qualities sought in new employees generally, and the qualities found in their older employees.[5] The two lists – with such traits as commitment, reliability, performance, and basic skills – corresponded remarkably.

There are strong correlations between work and health. People in poor health tend to leave the workforce earlier, have lower workforce participation rates, or are working part-time. Early retirees report more health problems than do workers of the same age, and 16 percent of non-employed older adults say that they are not working for health reasons. *People who stay on the job (or in equivalently intensive volunteer work) generally remain healthier and live longer, than those who do not.* They enjoy the psychological benefits of contribution, self-esteem and the social benefits of a diverse workplace community with its multi-cultural and generational exchanges.

A key question often raised is whether an older worker be as productive as a younger one, or not. The answer depends on the particular job and the nature of the individual performing it.[6] For example, electrical utilities anticipate a severe shortage of linemen when the current generation retires. The physical demands of climbing utility poles and stringing electrical cables cannot be met indefinitely, and many linemen devolve to less physically strenuous jobs several years before retiring. In healthcare, many nurses retire early or change jobs before retiring because of the physical and mental strains of the work – hence partly the cause of the current nursing staff shortage in developed countries. In aviation, research shows that older airline pilots perform as well as younger ones, and sixty-year-old pilots are the least likely to fail flight simulator tests.

U.S. commercial airline pilots are lobbying to drop the mandatory retirement age of sixty for their profession (or else extend it to sixty-five, on par with Europe and most of the world).[7] On the whole, jobs in increasingly knowledge and service economies are becoming less physical, so people of any age beyond adolescence can perform the overwhelming majority of knowledge-intensive jobs today.

Furthermore, people do not lose the insights of a lifetime over-night. Lee Iacocca has been reported as follows:[8] "I've always been against automated chronological dates to farm people out. The union would always say, make room for the new blood; there aren't enough jobs to go around. Well, that's a hell of a policy ... I don't know if the Internet will ... change stereotypes, but I hope so. I had people at Chrysler who were 40 but acted 80, and ... 80-year-olds who could do everything a 40-year-old can. You have to take a different view of age now. People are living longer. Age just gives experience. Besides, it takes you until about 50 to know what the hell is going on in the world."

It is evident that the traditional concepts of age and fitness should be drastically revised in an aging society, and especially concerning the aging workplace.

Mental Health Management of an Aging Workforce

The mental health of an aging workforce is crucial for maintaining and improving levels of creativity, mental agility and innovation for an enterprise. Besides the manipulation of work content – nature, flexibility and stimulation of tasks, which is often termed intervention towards 'meaningful' work – recent progress in cognitive neuroscience offers promise that aging minds can be mentally re-activated, in terms of attention, concentration, memory, and speed of mental grasping, linking and responding.

The fields of cognitive neuroscience in general, and more specifically the application of neuro-scientific methods and theories to the study of cognitive aging, have blossomed in the past decade, largely as the result of the development of functional magnetic resonance imaging (MRI) techniques. However, it is important to note that the use of neuro-imaging techniques to study brain and cognitive differences and changes during the adult lifespan has been on-going for the past several decades through the application of electrophysiological techniques, including the recording of electro-encephalographic activity (EEG) and event-related brain potentials (ERPs).[9] Clearly, much has been learned about age-related differences and changes in cognitive function and differences in the timing of mental processes from this earlier research.

Fluid or process-based mental abilities are largely independent of experience and instead depend on speed of processing, reasoning, and memory encoding and retrieval. These processes show substantial declines, in both cross-sectional and longitudinal studies, during the course of normal aging. On the other hand, it has generally been observed that knowledge-based or crystallized abilities (i.e. the extent to which a person has absorbed the contents of culture), such as verbal knowledge and comprehension, continue to be maintained or improve over the lifespan.[10]

In the cognitive aging literature, explanations for age-related declines in process-based or fluid abilities fall into two broad classes of theories. *General* or *common cause* explanations suggest that a common factor may be responsible for age-related declines – common factor models have suggested that a number of different factors including speed of processing, working memory, inhibition, or diminished sensory functions may be responsible for cognitive decline observed across a variety of different tasks.

An alternative to common factor models of cognitive aging are proposals that age-related cognitive decline is multifaceted with different processes changing across the adult lifespan at different rates. Support for these *specific factor* models has been provided by studies that have either equated younger and older adults' performance on some facets of a task, and observed changes in other facets of a task, or statistically controlled for general age-related changes and observed changes in other aspects of performance.

Experiments with both these approaches have shown that older adults have lesser capabilities in associations and memory, but that these can be changed by cognitive training interventions.[11] In some cases, older adults can achieve greater gains from formal cognitive training interventions than their younger counterparts. Aerobically trained older adults show improvements in both simple and highly complex cognitive tasks. *These results show that even relatively short exercise interventions can begin to restore some of the losses in brain volume and activity with normal aging.*

Take a Brain Fitness Course[12]

Michael Merzenich, a professor of neuroscience at the University of California at San Francisco, has provided new insights into the brain's ability to rearrange itself, or "plasticity", that offers potential for fighting e.g. senility and Alzheimer's. Experts in the past believed that the human being's gray matter was hardwired, that once a human reaches adulthood, the mind does little more than fade away. But in the mid-1980s Merzenich started to prove the opposite, that brains are "plastic," malleable, reprogrammable, capable of steady improvement through carefully designed exercises.

Brain plasticity, the field that Merzenich helped pioneer, is now one of the hottest areas in medicine, one with hugely positive implications for an aging society. Six years ago 450 million people, or 7% of the world's population, were over 65. By 2050, 16% of the world's population, nearly 1.5 billion people, will have turned 65. Almost half of Americans older than 85 develop Alzheimer's disease.

For Merzenich, improving memory and cognition among older people is just the beginning. Tweaked versions of his brain-fitness software serve the basis for several clinical trials that *Posit Science*, a company he co-founded in 2003 has underway for treating neurological diseases such as Alzheimer's and schizophrenia. "Most people think the solutions to the problems of aging will come from drugs, stem cells, genetic manipulation or medical devices," says Merzenich. "I believe this [work we're doing] is where the most benefit and the best answers will come from."

If brain research has proven anything, it is that a well-known cliché – use it or lose it – turns out to be a scientific fact. Unless neural connections are constantly challenged with new information, they will gradually weaken with age. Synapses once relied on for learning and memory produce less of the chemical neuromodulators used to ferry cognitive messages. An 80-year-old produces one-fifth the dopamine, a chemical strongly tied to attentiveness and memory, that a 20-year-old does. Without as much chemical lubrication, older brains begin failing to parse sounds or parts of conversations as they come tumbling out.

Neurological decline makes for what Merzenich calls a "noisy" brain. It's harder to hear and remember things. "All these things are going to waste because of disuse, unless you reenergize them by exercising the brain," he says.

Reading, going to work and navigating a busy life may be enough to maintain brain health, but increasing its performance takes massive amounts of practice – learning a new language, taking regular music lessons, doing complex jigsaw puzzles – to produce enough chemicals to make synapses stronger.

Merzenich built on his work to develop, with colleagues from UCSF, one of the first practical cochlear implants for the hearing-impaired, in the late 1980s. A cochlear implant is an external tiny microphone that transmits sound to surgically implanted electrodes that stimulate still-functioning auditory nerves in the inner ear. Patients who receive a cochlear implant need between 6 and 15 months to regain their hearing to the point where they say things sound normal. During that time, says Merzenich, as the patients listen to and repeat words they hear, their brains create new activity patterns to represent pieces of meaningful speech, thus teaching themselves to hear again. "I tried to tell the engineers the miracle is not the engineering, it is in the brain," says Merzenich. "Ultimately, it's as if the ear is replaced."

The possibilities of what the brain can do to heal itself are tantalizing. Merzenich envisions a day when everyone over 40 will take a brain fitness course that will enable his/her brain to retain information as well as it did when he/she was 20.

Boulton-Lewis proposes that, given time and sufficient motivation, older adults could achieve equivalent learning outcomes to younger learners.[13] Obviously, prior learning will make a difference in the ability of older adults to continue learning, and this is an important consideration for education generally. Motivation and confidence are critical to learning at any age, and particularly so in the aging workforce.

In the final instance, it comes down to managers providing, for an aging workforce, meaningful work, creating engaged workers, and enabling mentally-stimulating training and other interventions, assisted by new software developments. Dychtwald et. al. suggest the following common characteristics of interesting work:[14]

- *Stimulation*

  The work calls upon people to use their unique intellectual, creative, physical, and social skills and gifts, the very use of which stimulates and energizes them.

- *Variety*

  It offers variety and at least occasional challenges when the worker can improvise, invent, or improve products, services, business processes, and policies.

- *Edification*

  It involves learning new skills, honing existing ones, building new knowledge, and sharing it with others.

- *Connection*

  It fosters interaction with others in and outside the workplace, thereby cultivating a collaborative, supportive work environment.

- *Control*

  It provides a degree of control over the goals, methods, and timing of the activities performed or customers served.

- *Value*

  Inherently important and meaningful, the work clearly benefits an internal or external customer and sometimes even the community itself – especially when the worker can see the physical product or witness a customer enjoying a particular service.

When their work lacks these elements, employees tend to re-shape it or recast their roles, regardless of the job itself. A survey[15] conducted in 2004 indicated that only 20 percent of employees are genuinely engaged in their work and committed to their employers. Well under 50 percent say that their work includes collaboration with bright and experienced people, provides opportunities to learn and grow, or is worthwhile to society. Fewer than 50 percent say their workplace is congenial and fun, that employees cooperate and teamwork is the rule, or that people are respected for their abilities and can exercise them.

Two in five are looking to change careers or jobs. 42 percent feel burnout, and 33 percent find themselves at dead ends in their jobs, compared with 28 percent who are working on exciting new projects or assignments. Clearly, many more employees are engageable than are currently engaged.

Unlike the process reengineering focus and practices of the late 1980's and the early 1990's that largely ignored the human element, work practices of today should combine flexible technology with engaged and stimulated employees for an aging workforce.

The following box illustrates how Siemens AS, a Norwegian subsidiary of Siemens AG of Germany, implement initiatives to increase the mental health of its employees in the 55 to 64 age group.[16]

How Siemens AS Implement Mental Health Initiatives for Older Employees

Siemens AS is one of Norway's leading electro-mechanical companies and employs about 3,000 people at 26 sites throughout the country. About one-third of the employees are engineers or engineering scientists, and 84 % of the workforce is male. Siemens AS was established in Norway in 1898 and is a subsidiary company of the German enterprise, Siemens AG.

Towards the end of the 1980s the company became concerned about the aging of its workforce. There was hardly any internal mobility, some parts of the firm were in a steady market situation, and employees tended to stagnate in their jobs. The company wanted more mobility and development of employees, particularly among managerial staff. As a result, the company implemented a new career system in 1987, consisting of three main programs.

The three main programs initiated by Siemens AS were:

• *Constructive Management Mobility*

   The department of Management Development and Training initiated and implemented several actions, including the development of a training program for 'Constructive Management Mobility'. This program was established following advice from organizational psychologists and employee input. Mainly leaders in the 55 to 64 age group enrolled in the program. It consists of three two-day meetings over a period of eight months, with a mixture of plenary sessions, group work and individual work. Between the first and second meeting, a four-hour dialogue with an organizational psychologist takes place, focusing on individual interests, options and resources. Between the second and third meeting there is an exchange with the personnel director on alternative job opportunities in the company. Each program has 12 to 15 participants who belong to one of four small groups, so called "coaching groups", throughout the process. The members of each group are recruited from different divisions of the company.

- *TIPTOP – Senior Resource*

In 1993 a similar program for non-managerial staff was introduced: 'TIPTOP – Senior Resource'. It consists of two seminars lasting two days each, and three seminars lasting one day each. There are about three weeks between each seminar and the whole program takes four months. Non-managerial staff with more than 10 years of experience are invited. Each program has 12 to 15 participants and focuses on practical challenges at work and in the working situation. Its aim is to improve competence and to provide encouragement.

- *Active Reorientation Process*

In 1996, a reorientation program for all employees, irrespective of age, was started. This is a regular 1 to 2 day seminar for all employees, and is part of the effort to create a learning organization and to develop readiness for change.

Outcome

One year after completing the Constructive Management Mobility program, two-thirds of the participants experienced a major change in their job, i.e. they had new tasks or changed jobs. In some cases they moved to another division of the company. About 10 % found a new job outside the company and only 3 % took early retirement.

Participants report they have taken more responsibility for their own development, have increased their competence, and have become more open to change. The company considers participants to have improved their ability to work in teams, which they see as important for meeting future challenges.

The Constructive Management Mobility program has attracted interest from other companies and a few external participants were accepted for the 1998 program. Plans to establish this program as a separate business for external participants are under discussion.

Physical Health Management of an Aging Workforce

Mental and physical fitness are closely linked. Physical exercise stimulates blood flow, which keeps brain cells growing and prevents them from dying. As with mental fitness, physical fitness often comes down to a matter of exercising it or having it decline – this is true at any age.

Over time, repetitive tasks can lead to a variety of difficulties, including vision problems and headaches or back, muscle or joint pain. These conditions are not confined only to older workers. While some hearing loss may also be caused by continued exposure to noise or a one-time traumatic event, certain medical conditions, such as damage to the bone at the knee joint, may show up in older workers from either long-term exposure to certain workplace movements, involving bending or twisting the knee, or to recreational activities.

The ability to learn and use complicated and quick combinations of mental and motor skills, such as those needed to handle a joystick or other machine controls, decreases with age. In fact, it is believed that some rapid-reaction skills start to decline as early as age 30. In most cases, with the right physical exercise, perception, memory and learning skills remain constant well past the traditional retirement age of 65. There is even evidence that some mental abilities, such as use of language abilities and planning skills, improve with age. The ability to work well in groups and joining with other people's skills are abilities that tend to improve with age. With experience can come an improved understanding of tasks and work efficiency. This often means older workers learn to "work smarter," in emotional, mental and physical senses.

Advances in healthcare have brought vast improvements in people's health status at all ages. *People are starting to realize that they are far healthier than they expected to be as they age,* and the ailments that do afflict them can be alleviated if not eliminated. In fact, a majority of those over 55 are as healthy as people 10 years younger were a decade ago. For example, "the rate of disability among older Americans ... dropped from 26.2 percent in 1982 to 19.7 percent in 1999."[17] However, there are some problems with an older workforce that human resource departments will have to address. For example, Walter Maher of DaimlerChrysler Corporation notes that "it has become very clear that there is a priority in designing jobs in a way to reduce the risk of injury." He also points out that "standardized work practices are critical to injury prevention."[18] The following box illustrates Coors Brewing Company's health and wellness program.[19]

Coors Brewing Company's Health and Wellness Program

Coors Brewing Company presents a good example of a corporate culture that is focused on the health and wellness of its employees. As such, the company has had a measurable impact on productivity, particularly with its 5,000 employee workforce in the United States.

Coors employees have access to a full range of health and wellness resources for their use including a variety of fitness programs, a health coach, on-site physical therapy and medical center, a 25,000-square-foot wellness center and health risk appraisals that come with a $200 premium-reduction incentive. In addition, Coors has a transitional work program by which employees, managers and physicians create flexible options for employees to return to work.

"What we are using is a system that stresses prevention but also accommodates reaction to illness and injury that managers and employees can be comfortable with," says Eric Grobecker, human capital management manager for Coors Brewing.

The Coors model features impressive results:

- A 66 percent decrease between 2003 and 2004 in submitted long term disability claims

- A higher percentage of employees on long-term disability are returning to work within the first year.

"It's about creating a focused, yet flexible plan for managing productivity," says Grobecker.

The global healthcare industry – including pharmaceutical, biotechnology, medical devices and medical information technology – is making vast strides to assist the aging workforce. There is a growing convergence among these sectors, with an increasing rate of new products and speed-to-market, and lowering of medical product costs.

In "The Business of Healthcare Innovation" Kurt Kruger mentions that ... "In medical products, growth is sustainable because it is driven by demographic trends, the continued prevalence of diseases, and the fact that there is a near infinite capacity for absorbing medical technology within the practice of medicine."[20] He offers the example of implantable defibrillators, which monitor the heartbeat and give a potentially life-saving shock when needed: about 125,000 of the devices, at approximately $25,000 each, were implanted in the U.S. in 2003. Stents are another example: about 1.2 million bare-metal stents were implanted in the U.S. in 2002. Then along came drug-coated stents, designed to prevent the reclogging of arteries. The trend towards integrated drug-devise products, such as coated stents, is bound to increase. A combo device being used in back surgery involves a metal spine cage prepacked with a drug to promote bone growth.

Chronic Conditions of an Aging Workforce

Although chronic disability rates in the 65-plus population in the U.S. have been falling, with advancing age comes an increase in chronic health conditions.[21] For example, the rate of reported arthritis in the 1996 Health Interview Study in the U.S. was 50.1 per 1,000 persons in the population aged 18 to 44 but rose to 240.7 for persons between the ages of 45 and 64 and to 453.1 for the 65-to-74-age group. Nearly 30 percent of adults between the ages of 55 and 64, but only 5 percent of those aged 18 to 44, report having high blood pressure. Visual and especially hearing impairments also rise sharply with age.

Obesity is another common and physically limiting health problem experienced by millions of Americans of all ages. To the extent that obesity, alone or in conjunction with other health conditions, affects health and well-being, the trend is not encouraging. The percentage of adults with healthy weight has been declining, and obesity has been increasing, most notably among older men. Obesity also shows a tendency to increase with age up to about 65. In the 55-to-64-age group, more than 1 in 4 men and 1 in 3 women are considered obese.

While many chronic conditions are not necessarily debilitating and can be alleviated with medication, assistive devices, improved diet, and/or exercise, some conditions can significantly limit an individual's ability to perform certain tasks of daily living. Over one-fifth of people between the ages of 55 and 64 report some limitation in activity due to chronic conditions, a figure that rises to nearly one-third in the 65-to-74 population.

Although the above-mentioned statistics might raise questions about the work ability of many middle-aged and older individuals, the fact that people report less than excellent health or some limitation in activity does not mean they are incapable of doing any work. Many individuals with chronic health conditions are indeed in the labor force, and many others could likely remain gainfully employed, perhaps in a modified work environment or on a reduced work schedule.

As the workforce continues to age, employers can expect an increase in the number of workers with chronic conditions. Work-related accidents fail to show a comparable age-related increase, but when work injuries occur to older workers, they tend to be more severe than those experienced by younger workers. Although work injury rates for older workers are lower, they are more costly to treat or compensate when they do occur.

The number of workers with serious health problems could rise if many of the less healthy workers who in the past have tended to retire early decide to postpone retirement, perhaps as a result of increases in the normal retirement age or reductions in early retirement incentive programs. Employers can gain insight into where workforce interventions and risk management strategies might prove fruitful from age audits of their workforce, as well as from assessments of workers (e.g. transportation workers) at particular risk, rather than directed toward specific age groups or individuals.

Health Plans[22]

Employers have four basic choices when considering using their physical healthcare plans to deliver some (or all) of their health promotion programs to an aging workforce:

(1) They can do nothing and hope that healthcare costs do not increase and that the health of their employees stays stable;

(2) They can operate their own health promotion programs, thus fully controlling their own destiny;

(3) They can transfer their responsibility for preventing disease to their health plans and hope the providers do a good job; and

(4) They can share the responsibility with their health plans. This fourth option is often a strategy that is efficacious and cost-efficient for both parties.

Health plans for an aging workforce have a health promotion dilemma. On one hand, as employers agree to more "managed care capitated" arrangements (thus assuming more financial risk), there is an incentive to prevent disease through health promotion. On the other hand, as costs become more tightly controlled, it is difficult to spare the resources necessary to provide effective health promotion services, especially given that the return on investment is often several years away. Therefore, if health plans are to be used as a resource in the delivery of worksite health promotion programs, their services must be chosen carefully with attention to quality assurance. The health promotion professional must also recognize that these services may not be delivered cost free.

Services that health plans can provide for an aging workforce include the following:

• Health-risk assessments

• Targeted health interventions such as disease management, high-risk interventions, and individual case management

• Consumerism assistance such as nurse lines, medical self-care, and audio health libraries

• Health promotion classes or seminars.

Designing Health Promotion Programs

The health promotion programs that are best practices (those using innovative, imaginative ideas with the potential to improve business results) are systematically planned and comprehensive in nature. Successful programs blend a wide range of program offerings with cultural and environmental support to make the greatest impact and include four important cornerstones:[23]

a) Needs assessment and evaluation

b) Effective interventions

c) Relapse prevention

d) Healthy culture development

These four cornerstones (or components) are interrelated. For instance, needs assessment and evaluation directly determine what intervention programs are needed and identify what can be done to develop a healthy culture. In turn, the results of these activities are assessed through needs assessment and evaluation. Likewise, relapse prevention and its success helps determine appropriate interventions and must be supported by a healthy culture. Each of the four cornerstones has a relationship to the others, either supporting them, being supported by them, or both.

A number of avenues are available for the health promotion program planner to obtain needs assessment and evaluation data. Some data are available directly through health promotion program initiatives such as health-risk appraisals or employee interest surveys.

Other data must be obtained through collaboration with human resources, benefits, occupational health, or workers' compensation departments within the enterprise. Further, some data, while not a direct measure of an enterprise's specific employee population, can be obtained through various county, state, and federal health agencies.

Systematic evaluation should be conducted to determine health promotion program needs and to assess the progress of any ongoing activities, and meeting the established goals and objectives. Evaluation involves initial and periodic needs analysis and quality review as well as the longitudinal assessment of program results. The information obtained from evaluation can be used to establish the program design, develop it further, improve it, and/or to optimize the desired outcomes, and to provide information to justify sustaining the program and enhancing its growth and evolution.

Needs analysis determines the needs and interests of the people and the enterprise being served. This information can then be used in selecting programs, within the constraints of budget. Program evaluation usually involves the assessment of process, impact, and outcomes. Additionally, value analysis is often conducted to determine the overall value of the health promotion program. These activities can be summarized as follows:

- *Value analysis* determines which health promotion program produces the greatest benefit for the lowest cost. A relative value can accordingly be established for each program. This information can be used in selecting future programs, within the constraints of budget.

- *Process evaluation* analyzes the qualitative aspects of program delivery, such as enrollment, participant satisfaction, and effect of mode of delivery on participation. Periodic quality assurance checks related to providers, equipment, and program operation and delivery should also be included in the process evaluation.

- *Impact evaluation* assesses the immediate behavioral, attitudinal, knowledge, and cultural changes that occur as a result of the program. Examples include lifestyle behavior changes, level-of-readiness for behavior change, and changes in health beliefs.

- *Outcome evaluation* determines the success of the program in affecting health-related outcomes such as health status indexes, morbidity and mortality. It can also be used to examine the program's effect on economic outcomes such as productivity, absenteeism, workers compensation claims, and healthcare utilization. Economic outcome evaluation involves cost-effectiveness, cost savings and cost-benefit ratio analyses.

The above-mentioned physical health management pointers for an aging workforce are only a broad outline. For comprehensive approaches and applications the reader is urged to consult the sources listed in the references to this chapter.

Emotional Health Management of an Aging Workforce

It seems without doubt that older workers and managers change over time and show different behavior or attitude compared to younger employees. However, findings about what the specific emotional differences are that older workers develop in terms of experience, shift of motivational basis or performance behavior, are scarce and ambiguous. Nevertheless, considering the significant demographic trends now being evidenced, older employees will play an increasing role for the success of their companies in the future.

It is therefore crucial to understand the emotional specifics of their performance and productivity levels, as well as the organizational and societal conditions that support or hinder productive engagement, and to appropriately intervene to improve the mental health of an aging workforce. One way of analyzing this is within the framework of organizational energy.[24] Workers of any age can experience emotional or psychological stress in the workplace, affecting organizational energy negatively. While older workers deal better with certain types of emotions, they face other emotional health challenges than younger workers.

While there are many potential sources of workplace stress, some causes of stress might be more specific to older workers. For example:

- Feeling threatened by younger workers or supervisors
- Coping with negative attitudes about aging
- Concerns about retirement plans.

Individuals react to and cope with stressful situations in different ways. No matter what the source, stress reduces workers' effectiveness and ability to concentrate on work. Symptoms of stress, such as the following, can affect health and safety:

- A rise in blood pressure or pulse

- Rapid breathing

- Upset stomach

- Headaches

- Muscle tension (including tightened abdominal muscles).

Managers and supervisors should know the signs of workplace stress and look for ways to help workers control and manage it. Managing conflict on the job is one way to lessen workplace stress.

Organizational energy has previously in this chapter been defined as the force a company purposefully works with – it reflects the extent to which an organization has mobilized its emotional, cognitive and behavioral potential in pursuit of its goals. For most of the 21st century, management theory and practice have adopted a technical, analytical approach in which the role of the so-called soft factors, like emotions and feelings, has largely been ignored.

Both academics and managers are recognizing the powerful role that emotions play in shaping corporate behavior. The real challenge, however, is to link emotions to performance goals and objectives. The leadership task is not just to make people happy in the hope that happy people will do the right things, but to ensure that the company's vision and strategy capture people's emotional excitement, engage their intellectual capacities, and produce a sense of urgency for taking action. In essence, it is seen as a task of unleashing organizational energy and marshaling it in support of key strategic goals.

In a state of productive organizational energy, aging employees have channeled their emotions, awareness and effort towards pursuing shared company goals. Employees are driven, fully engaged and committed to the accomplishment of the collective unit's core activities. *Comfortable inertia* can be characterized by low positive energy, and the main characteristics of aging workforces falling in this state are satisfaction and contentment with the status quo. This is combined with a low activity level, people not being mentally alert, and low emotional tension.

Resignative (including apathetic) *inertia* can be described as a situation when aging workforces have only partially mobilized their potential, with older employees' positive interests in the company goals consequently being low. Negative emotions including boredom and disappointment would be dominant and accompanied by distanced or lethargic behavior. Older employees with negative-aggressive energy conditions show a high degree of activity, alertness and emotional involvement. But this mobilized potential is negatively oriented toward the organization, other units or employee groups. This is accompanied by destructive behavior, e.g. creating conflict and distrust, or is visible in emotional expressions such as anger, anxiety and hatred.

To understand the engagement, energy and performance behavior of older workforces, the reasons why some older workers experience productive energy, while others go through phases of inertia, resignation and burnout, or tend toward destructive emotions and behavior, must be identified. The aim is to target those underlying factors that influence the energy of aging workforces, i.e. distinct drivers of engagement and dedication of older workforces based on a model of organizational energy. *A model of organizational energy proposes that meaningfulness, collective efficacy, autonomy, impact, collective commitment, cohesion and inspiring leadership behavior are responsible for productive organizational energy* (Figure 7.1).[25]

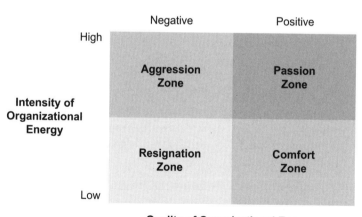

Figure 7.1
Four organizational energy zones

In Figure 7.1, organizational energy is related but not identical to the sum of the energy of individuals. Individual energy, especially of leaders, influences organizational energy, and the energy state of the organization affects the energy of individuals. Companies differ in both intensity and quality of energy. Intensity refers to the strength of organizational energy as seen in the level of activity, the amount of interaction, the extent of alertness and the extent of emotional excitement. Symptoms of low energy are often obvious: apathy and inertia, tiredness, inflexibility and cynicism. Qualitatively, organizational energy can be characterized as positive or negative energy (fear, frustration or sorrow). In fact, it is the intersection of intensity and quality that determines an organization's energy state, which usually falls into one of four categories:

- Companies in the *comfort zone* have low animation and a relatively high level of satisfaction. With weak but positive emotions such as calmness and contentedness, they lack the vitality, alertness and emotional tension necessary for initiating bold new strategic thrusts or significant change.

- Companies in the *resignation zone* demonstrate weak, negative emotions – frustration, disappointment and sorrow. People suffer from lethargy and feel emotionally distant from company goals. They lack excitement or hope.

- Companies in the *aggression zone* experience internal tension founded on strong, negative emotions. Tension drives their intensely competitive spirit, which manifests itself in high levels of activity and alertness – and focused efforts to achieve company goals.

- In the *passion zone*, companies thrive on strong, positive emotions – joy and pride in the work. Employees' enthusiasm and excitement mean that attention is directed toward shared organizational priorities.

An aging workforce holds the potential threat – to all enterprises – of negative and weak emotions. In essence, positive and high levels of organizational energy create the necessary combination of cognitive, emotional and action-taking capabilities, and align the resulting forces to achieve business goals. That is the reason why, *without a high level of positive energy, a company cannot achieve radical productivity improvements, cannot grow fast, and cannot cre-*

ate major innovations. Enterprise leaders must acknowledge this simple reality, and focus explicit attention on how they can harness and unleash the energy their organizations need if they are going to achieve the kind of performance they seek with an aging workforce.

Leadership behavior towards older employees is an important aspect for generating organizational energy and required performance behavior of older workforces. Negative beliefs of managers about their older people influence their behavior in a way that they give less attention and feedback to older employees, and provide less support for career development, retraining and promotion. This, in turn, holds the risk of being a self-fulfilling prophecy and to develop into a negative downward spiral of older employee behavior. It explains the reason why older employees often feel distrustful and defensive, thinking they are deficient as being 'too old'. Negative energy states of low intensity often result, which should not mean that older employees are not able to perform energetically; they just might not experience the necessary positive influencing factors, e.g. appropriate and supporting leadership behavior to develop and provide their full strengths.

Integrated Health Management Tools to Increase Productivity and Creativity of an Aging Workforce

In view of the interrelated dimensions of mental, physical and emotional health of employees, and the critical challenges of an aging workforce in all three of these, it is essential – besides individual measures in each dimension – to have integrated tools for their effective joint management. Two such tools are presented here: an *Integrated Health Performance* framework (IHP), and the *Workability Index.*

An Integrated Health Performance framework is illustrated in Figure 7.2.

In an increasingly knowledge-networked innovation economy, and in view of the significant demographic trends, the greater focus will in future be on integrated health management for higher levels of creativity

	Productivity (for Efficiency)	Creativity (for Innovation)
Mental Health	*Focus* Improving the Mousetrap	*Focus* Creating & Developing a New Mouse-Catching Device
Physical Health	*Focus* Physical Strength and Endurance (Existing Technologies)	*Focus* Physical Flexibility and Dexterity (New Technologies)
Emotional Health	*Focus* Consistency of Self-Application and Self-Esteem	*Focus* Positive and High Energy Levels

Figure 7.2
Integrated health performance network

– to enable innovative competitiveness and sustainability of enterprises.

Table 7.1 illustrates another important type of integrated health management tool – the Workability Index.[26]

Workability is a relatively new concept describing the balance between human resources and work life characteristics. Human resources include health and functional capacities (physical, mental, emotional), knowledge, skills and competence, as well as values, attitudes and motivation. The work life parameters include work content, work demands (physical, mental, emotional), work environment, work community, work organization as well as management and leadership. Workability can be assessed with Work Ability Index (WAI) developed by the Finnish Institute of Occupational Health.[27] The range of WAI varies from 7 to 49 points, and is classified into poor (7 to 27), moderate (28 to 36), good (37 to 43) and excellent (44 to 49 points). Long-term studies over 11 years have shown that WAI change with age, at least after the age of 51 years. About 30% of subjects reported WAI to decline at least by 10 points, about 10% reported an improvement of at least 3 points, and among 60% of subjects the WAI remained on the base line level during 11 years. The changes were independent of type of work and gender. The changes in WAI with age describe the increasing diversity of human workability during aging.

The main reasons for the increased diversity in workability are due to the changes in health and functional capacities as well as work life parameters. Promotion of workability during aging is the key concept to prevent the decline of workability. The results and experiences since the early 1990s have shown that an integration of processes improving the health and competences together with work environment and work community matters create the best results. As a consequence, work quality and productivity will improve, as well as the well-being and quality of life of individuals.

The Workability Index is an instrument currently in use in especially occupational healthcare. It can be used at an early stage of

Table 7.1
Workability Index

The Workability Index covers seven items, each of which is evaluated with the use of one or more questions:	
Item 1	Current workability compares with the lifetime best
Item 2	Workability in relation to the demand of the job
Item 3	Number of the current diseases diagnosed by a physician
Item 4	Estimated work impairment due to diseases
Item 5	Sick leave during the past year
Item 6	Own prognosis of workability two years from now
Item 7	Mental resources
Each item has its own score, and the best rating on the index is 49 points and the worst is 7 points. The points can be divided into four different categories:	
poor	7 – 27 points
moderate	28 – 36 points
good	37 – 43 points
excellent	44 – 49 points

career development to help ensure that the correct measures are taken to maintain workability. In its application the data remain confidential, and on an individual level the information is only used for occupational healthcare purposes. The Workability Index is a relatively easy and quick tool, and can be used for follow-up studies both at an individual and at group levels.

The basis of workability is health in the sense of physical, psychological and social functional capacity. This integrated health concept is applied through education and skills plus motivational and attitudinal factors to produce the resources available to the individual.

These individual resources are then tested by the mental and physical demands of the job plus the demands and challenges of the working environment and the workplace community. Deficiencies in skills weaken the individual's resources, and when the individual is unable to properly meet the demands of the job, there is a danger of workability being undermined by fatigue and burnout. Thus, besides being the interactive sum of many different factors, an individual's 'final' workability is also the result of a process over time. Workability is at the same time always a component of the individual's overall life status at any given moment.

In conclusion, compared to their younger colleagues, older workers have many strengths that impact positively on productivity and creativity. These include a superior ability to solve problems, the ability to take a broad view and understand how things interrelate, the ability to avoid mistakes, a sense of responsibility, initiative, a strong work ethic and a sense of commitment to their work, and the ability to take others into consideration.

In a business-economic sense, aging worker realities highlight the importance of several interrelated health and business performance factors. *In essence, we can say that the aging of a company's personnel represents an opportunity if we can just learn how to take advantage of it.* There are many ways we can support the workability of aging employees, including changing management practices and attitudes, improving the working environment and the planning of work, and encouraging employees to take up physical, mental and emotional exercises and/or activities.

Key Pointers of Chapter 7

- Health is much more than just a physical issue concerning an aging workforce – it is an integrated, interlinked issue of mental, physical and emotional elements.

- Fitness is not a matter of age – younger workers can be less fit than older workers, despite the fact that physical and cognitive abilities slowly diminish as part of the natural aging process. With modern scientific advances, and the right managerial interventions, this process can often be reversed and maintained for workers well into their 70's.

- Mental health of aging workers can be improved through e.g. 'brain-fitness' software and managerial programs such as constructive management mobility and active reorientation processes.

- Physical health of an aging workforce can be improved through targeted health plans and designed health promotion programs, in collaboration with the growing global healthcare industry.

- Emotional health of an aging workforce can best be understood within the framework of positive and high levels of organizational energy. Leadership behavior plays a crucial role in generating and maintaining such energy levels among its aging workforce.

- Two integrated health management tools are:
  - an Integrated Health Performance (IHP) framework
  - a Workability Index.

  It is essential to utilize integrated tools because of the interrelationships among the three major health management dimensions.

8 The Fourth V-Field: Work Environment Approaches for the Aging Workforce

Key Issues of this Chapter

- The importance of appropriate work environment and physical tools for an aging workforce
- Work environment responses to physical changes of an aging workforce
- Ergonomics and reduction of stress in the workplace
- Creating the right work environment platforms and processes
- Technology and tools for an aging workforce

The Importance of Appropriate Work Environment and Physical Tools for an Aging Workforce

The existing work environments of most enterprises are not adjusted to the needs of elderly workers, and many elderly workers are not adequately oriented or trained to cope with new technologies or alternative tools for their easy use or convenient accessibility. With a rapidly aging workforce, the importance of appropriate work environments, new sets of working models, and sound orientation and training in new technologies and tools are crucial.

A new set of work environment models – in terms of working time, work space, content, structure, workplace design, work tools, organizational structure, and support by new technologies – are becoming available through various programs. One such program is RESPECT, an EU funded research project to enable new approaches and tools to re-orientate employers and employees, and offer new tools.[1] Different partners from research institutions and enterprises worked together in the framework of the

EU project "Research action for improving Elderly workers Safety, Productivity, Efficiency and Competency Toward the new 'working environment' (RESPECT)". The project is promoted in the program of "Quality of Life and Management of Living Resources".

In the following box, the importance of an appropriate work environment, in conjunction with other measures, are illustrated by way of a Swedish steel company's experience.[2]

SSAB Tunnplat: Work Environment and Related Initiatives

SSAB Tunnplat (Svenkst Stål AB Strip Products) is part of Swedish Steel (SSAB) and consists of two steel plants located in Luleå and Borlänge in Sweden.

SSAB Tunnplat's interest in aging employees began over 15 years ago when a research study found that early retired workers had much better physical and mental health than those still working. In this context, the company focused their attention on how to improve health and well-being of older workers.

SSAB Tunnplat's initiatives addressed three main areas:

- *Improvements of work environment and individual health check-ups*

  Workplace lighting was improved, sight examinations were provided and employees were given spectacles for specialized work. Conference rooms were equipped with hearing loops for the hearing impaired and ergonomically unsuitable working places were rebuilt. Special devices for packaging steel coils and sheets, and for driving overhead cranes were introduced. These measures were combined with rotation at different work stations to avoid overstraining individual workers' muscles, joints and ligaments. Initiatives aimed at improving the general health of employees included individual health check-ups and rehabilitation.

- *Age dependent ability for shift work*

  Attention was given to understanding the different attitudes towards shift work between older and younger employees. Older workers often prefer few night shifts in succession, while younger workers generally have no difficulty with working night shifts. Thus, it is important to create an understanding between the age groups by making the young and old both grasp the different environmental demands that shift work could mean for them.

- *Union initiatives*

    The unions and the workers introduced several working teams aimed at constructing a good shift schedule taking into consideration older workers. The schedule was ultimately decided through a democratic process, including a trial run of each proposed schedule, an employee questionnaire, and an employee vote.

In addition to the ergonomic optimization of the workplace, the individual health service, and good shift schedules, the option for older employees – at least from the age of 58 – to reduce working hours was recognized as an important measure to keep these employees at work up to regular retirement age. Employers were rather reluctant to reorganize work to allow half-time work but, over time, state regulations grew more flexible and the attitude of the company has softened. As a result, many older employees were able to work up to the regular retirement age.

Work Environment Responses to Physical Changes of an Aging Workforce

It is important to understand the physical changes of an aging workforce to be able to plan and respond appropriately, in terms of what employers need to do to change the work environment, and also what workers need to know about themselves in terms of work environments. Table 8.1 provides a list of appropriate work environment responses to physical changes of an aging workforce, relating to workers' muscles, bones, cardiovascular and respiratory systems, hearing, skin, mental processes, and sensory and motor processes.[3]

Table 8.1

Work environment responses to physical changes of an aging workforce

How organs and systems change with age	How age-related changes impact work	What employers need to do	What workers need to do
Muscles			
Muscle strength gradually declines, reaching an annual average three percent decline after age 70. On average, those 51 to 55 have about 80 per cent of the strength they had in their early 30s. Muscles lose elasticity. Muscles take longer to respond.	Less muscle strength and endurance may affect the ability to do physical work over extended periods, particularly for heavy or intense activities. Though maximum strength declines with age, the level of strength available necessary for most work does not change greatly; grip strength decreases.	Provide mechanical devices and power tools for lifting and moving. Minimize lifting by: • storing at lower levels • packing in smaller quantities or containers. Provide supportive, adjustable seating and workstations. Minimize work requiring fixed (static) muscle positions.	Use the equipment provided for lifting and moving loads. Maintain proper posture. Reduce or eliminate upper-body twisting. Wear proper footwear. Change position frequently. Stretch before, during and after work.
Bones			
Bones lose calcium, making them more porous. This can lead to osteoporosis. Cartilage (padding between bones) deteriorates and can lead to bone damage at the joint.	More porous, less dense bones are more likely to break as a result of workplace slips or falls. Work injuries may result from short-term overexertion or repeated, long-term stress on muscles, joints and bones.	Minimize slips, trips and falls by reducing climbing and not working at height. Arrange for proper equipment and tools storage. Supply safe ladders and steps. Ensure proper lighting.	Use ladder properly and be cautious on steps. Add weight-bearing activities (walking, running) to a regular exercise routine. Eat a healthy diet, including foods containing calcium.

Table 8.1 (continued)
Work environment responses to physical changes of an aging workforce

How organs and systems change with age	How age-related changes impact work	What employers need to do	What workers need to do
Cardiovascular and respiratory systems			
The heart, lungs and the circulatory system's ability to carry oxygen-filled blood decreases. Between age 30 and 65, functional breathing capacity is reduced by 40 %. Blood vessels lose flexibility. Arteries thicken, which can lead to hardening of the arteries, increasing the risk of high blood pressure and strokes.	Capacity for extended physical labor is reduced. Changes do not usually affect normal work. Lessened blood flow to outer parts of the body reduces heat loss from skin surface in hot conditions. Insufficient warm clothing can lead to frostbite and hypothermia.	Avoid work in extreme heat or cold, if possible. Adjust work in high or low temperatures. Provide air conditioning, heating and adequate ventilation. Assign and schedule work to avoid fatigue.	Avoid over-fatigue. Dress properly for hot and cold conditions. Use appropriate personal protective equipment (including masks and respirators). Maintain a healthy lifestyle by: • controlling weight • not smoking • avoiding substance abuse • eating properly; exercising.
Hearing			
The ability to hear and distinguish one kind of sound from another, especially high-pitched sounds, decreases with age. More difficulty locating the source of sounds	Hearing loss may reduce the ability to hear alarms and other work-related signals, as well as verbal instructions.	Reduce general workplace noise. Use back-up warning systems, lights and vibration systems (vibrating pagers) along with sounds. Reduce long-term and repeated exposure to noise.	Use personal protective equipment to preserve hearing. Have hearing tested. Use hearing aids if prescribed.

Table 8.1 (continued)

Work environment responses to physical changes of an aging workforce

How organs and systems change with age	How age-related changes impact work	What employers need to do	What workers need to do
Vision			
Flexibility of the lens of the eye changes, often resulting in long-sightedness, which is noticeable around age 40. The eye's ability to see light gradually diminishes. The amount of light reaching the back of the eye can decline by up to 75 per cent between ages 20 and 50.	Visual changes may affect the ability to read printed material, dials and screens within arm's length. Ability to do detailed tasks may be affected. Ability to adapt to changing lighting conditions may be reduced.	Where practical, improve workplace lighting, making it individually adjustable and suited to the task. Reduce glare by using several light sources rather than one large source. Provide indirect lighting. Avoid sharp contrasts in light levels.	Have vision tested regularly and get reading glasses if required. Use personal protective equipment for eyes.
Skin			
The skin stretches less easily. Secretion of oil and sweat declines.	Decreased tolerance to heat and cold.	Control or limit work in extreme heat or cold.	Use skin protection, lotions and protective clothing.
Mental processes			
While mental processes are at their height when people are in their 30s and 40s, these abilities decline only very slightly in the 50s and 60s. A decline may not be noticeable until people are 70 or older.	It may take slightly longer to process information. In most situations, changes do not affect work performance.	Reduce multi-tasking. Increase time between steps of a task. Increase available decision-making time. Reinforce tasks and skills (including emergency response) through repetition, drills and refresher courses.	Exercise to increase flow of blood, which encourages growth, and prevents or reduces death of brain cells. Follow a healthy diet; get enough sleep. Minimize stress at and outside work. Challenge the brain through hobbies, reading and other mentally stimulating activities.

Table 8.1 (continued)
Work environment responses to physical changes of an aging workforce

How organs and systems change with age	How age-related changes impact work	What employers need to do	What workers need to do
	Sensory and motor processes		
The sensory system carries messages to the brain and the motor control system carries messages from the brain to parts of the body performing an activity. A decrease in the size and flexibility of muscles and a reduction in central and outer nerve fibres occur with age.	Lengthened reaction and response time may slow decision-making in some cases. Except where extremely quick responses are required, these changes do not affect the ability to perform most work.	Reduce multi-tasking. Provide opportunities to practice and reinforce tasks.	Practice and reinforce tasks.

Creating a Safe and Healthy Work Environment

Workplace hazards affect the health and safety of workers of all ages. Although age doesn't make a difference to a worker's health and safety requirements, certain hazards, if not dealt with, may present added dangers to older workers. For example, poor or inadequate lighting may pose a particular safety issue for older workers. However, improving lighting will also help ensure the health and safety of all workers.

Sudden-onset injuries are likely to occur to workers of any age when they:

- Do not recognize a hazard.
- Do not have their eyes or mind on the task.
- Are in the line of fire when something goes wrong.
- Are participating in an activity that may cause them to lose their balance, grip or traction.
- Are rushing, frustrated or careless.
- Are unable to react quickly enough to avoid injury, possibly because they are in poor physical condition.

When managers and supervisors in a workplace adopt supportive attitudes toward older workers, their abilities and their health and safety, it has a positive impact on everyone's attitude toward aging. Supervisors should communicate directly and honestly with workers about health and safety concerns and should be aware of what options the employer can offer in connection with worker health and safety. For instance, if the worker is sick or has health concerns, the supervisor should know whether the employer can offer time off work, part-time work, workplace aids, or assistance or changes in assignments.

Ergonomics and Reduction of Stress for an Aging Workforce in the Workplace

Ergonomics is the science and practice of integrating human resources (workers) with particular work environments, for optimum long-term productivity and effectiveness of an enterprise. In the following box an ergonomics strategy example of Dow Safety and Industrial Hygiene is provided.[4] As in any large manufacturing industry, musculoskeletal injuries and illnesses contribute to higher healthcare costs and decreased productivity.

Musculoskeletal Ergonomics Strategy (MES) of Dow

Dow Safety and Industrial Hygiene has been tracking incidences and severity (above and beyond OSHA required information) of musculoskeletal disorders of its workers, as well as designing strategies to minimize their incidence and impact, for years. At the same time, their health promotion has been offering a variety of awareness and educational programs designed to address this need. The data gathered through these efforts, combined with the results of the analysis, led to Dow's Health Targets, resulting in the current cross-functional initiative for managing musculoskeletal disorders.

To address this issue, a team was chartered that was made up of representatives from industrial hygiene, safety, health promotion, and occupational health services. The vision for this team was to create a standardized process that would identify and prioritize key risk factors associated with musculoskeletal injuries and illnesses within Dow and reduce their incidence through prevention and intervention efforts coordinated across health and safety disciplines. The design elements of this strategy included integration of activities at the local level as guided through a multidisciplinary team, standardizing activities through identification of best practices, and a comprehensive approach to risk control activities. Built into the approach are ongoing data analysis and program validation. The two major components of this program are as follows:

Action	Result
Risk identification	• Development and identification of tools for self-identification of ergonomic risk and early symptoms • Delivery mechanism and implementation process • Data collection and analysis • Integration with the Dow Health Surveillance • Program to identify potential at-risk individuals
Intervention efforts	• Health counseling for at-risk individuals • Consultation with plants and businesses on potential administrative and engineering controls, and job restrictions • Ergonomic related programs and activities offered through health promotion • Physical preparedness (fitness for duty) programs administered through the occupational health department

To design and develop new ergonomic models for an aging workforce the approach of the EU project RESPECT proposes the following guidelines.[5]

a) *Better use of work environment knowledge and experience of employees*

Companies, who are not aware of the work environment abilities of advanced employees, spend a lot of money for qualifications they might already have in the company. The companies should give their advanced professionals the possibility to bring in their work environment experiences by experience sharing, by creation of intergenerational teams, and by building up experience and knowledge in fields outside of the own function, within previously defined timeframes.

b) Ergonomic-adjusted short breaks

Older workers need more time to recover from strain than younger ones. The need for recovery increases with age and heaviness of the work. Companies should introduce short breaks for older workers who have to do physical work.

Pre-planned short breaks (e.g. after 55 minutes of work 5 minutes break or after 110 minutes of work 10 minutes break) have been introduced for workers in the automobile assembly line in the region of Baden-Wuerttemberg in Germany. The positive effect in physically or mentally demanding jobs has first been demonstrated in recent studies showing that short breaks (3-minutes break for every 27 minutes of work or 9-minutes break for every 51 minutes of work) increased the production rate and reduced the discomfort ratings.

c) Ergonomic-adjusted reduction of working time

Reduced health and functional capacities can mean that an older worker cannot work eight hours anymore at a workplace with a high physical load. If it is not possible to reduce the work load by means of changing the work contents or work methods in very demanding jobs, workers should have the option to reduce hours.

In a German glass-processing company a continuous shift system was introduced. As some of the older workers wanted to work part-time within the new shift system an integrated optional working time model in the continuous shift system was implemented. The advantages of the new model are: The workers have the choice to reduce their working time, dependent e.g. on their health status or preference. The workers remain in the team in which they have worked for many years (in other companies a reduction of working time can only be realized by changing from shift work to day work. The new shift system corresponds to ergonomic recommendations for the design of shift systems.

d) Training of particular muscles and instruction about correct lifting and handling of heavy weights

Despite increasing levels of automation, many blue collar workers, e.g. in the automobile industry, have to lift and handle heavy weights. On an average the muscle strength increases up to the age of 20 to 30 years; thereafter without training muscle strength decreases with age. Therefore working in unfavorable working conditions may cause negative effects on health such as backache or even skeletal diseases.

Besides ergonomic improvements of the workplace the behavior and capacities of the individual should be improved. Many workers do not know how to lift and handle heavy weights correctly to avoid negative effects on the spine.

- Therefore one very important preventive measure is to instruct the workers at the workplace and to monitor their behavior in intervals.

- A second preventive intervention is a newly developed method to train those belly and dorsal muscles which are acting directly at the spine. This is a 3 minutes maximum power-training, with new developed special equipment.

e) Shift system designed according to ergonomic recommendations

Shift work may have many negative effects on sleep, fatigue, performance, appetite, health and social life. Shift systems designed according to ergonomic recommendations may reduce these problems. This is of particular importance for older shift workers (> 45 years) because they tend to have more such problems than younger ones. Change from old traditional shift system to new shift system which, for example, has a quick forward rotation of shifts will bring positive effects to elderly workers.

f) Train the trainer

Many companies do not consider the ergonomic characteristics and needs of elderly workers by offering and preparing their vocational training programs. So it is important that trainers and those responsible for the personnel department know about this and are adequately prepared to monitor, assess, respond and measure these programs.

Creating the Right Work Environment Action Fields

Based upon the above work ergonomy pointers, seven work environment action fields are identified:

(1) Leadership actions

Managers should be aware of the workplace abilities of their elderly employees. They should learn how to assign employees to workplace according to their performance, how to redesign workplaces; how to integrate employees into permanent or project teams, and how to improve the exchange of experience and intergenerational communication. Finally, they should make full use of the innovative potential of their elderly staff.

(2) Use of expert knowledge

As a worker gets older, the experience-related workplace knowledge increases. Companies have to learn to use the professional competence of their elderly staff, to facilitate the informal transfer of knowledge, and to improve inter-generational communication.

(3) Working time actions

First, shift systems should follow ergonomic recommendations in their design. Second, there is a need to individualize the working-time conditions of elderly workers. Individual health conditions and personal interests require flexible assignments. Increased use of innovative working-time models could improve both productivity and customer orientation as well as providing a motivation for elderly workers for their transition into retirement.

(4) Recruitment policies

Governmental legislation generally calls for creating and preserving job opportunities for elderly workers. State agencies and companies should support the targeted recruitment of elderly employees and experienced specialists with workplace demands in mind.

(5) Project work

It is important to use all kinds of job modifications (job enlargement, job enrichment, job rotation, group work) to motivate elderly workers. Furthermore, companies should promote responsibility and self-control among elderly workers and use more flexible work organization schemes (project management, job sharing, telework).

(6) Human resources development

There is a need to reform corporate training programs aimed at different types of workplaces. Trainers should use age-specific didactics (learning speed/content, learning fear/restraints) and set up age-heterogeneous or homogeneous learning groups according to learning requirements. Courses for elderly workers should be practice-orientated and based directly on the workplace demands of, for e.g., product development processes.

(7) Public relations

On the societal level, co-operation between companies and institutions should be improved. People should be informed about the knowledge and abilities of elderly employees and changing workplace requirements (posters, internet, brochures, information centers, congresses, fairs, seminars).

From the above-mentioned it can be seen that the seven work environment action fields cover all V-fields in this book, and are therefore closely interrelated; indeed, each of the five V-fields in the book are interrelated with the others. The growing part of elderly workers in the active population and the looming lack of specialists force companies to take measures how to ergonomically improve the power of innovation and productivity of their staff. The prior aim of all activities should be the sensitization of the management and of the workforce for the excellence of elder workers in appropriate work environments.

The following box illustrates how some organizations make ergonomic adjustments for an aging workforce.[6]

How Some Organizations Implement Ergonomic Adjustments for Aging Workers

Hazenberg Construction, a Dutch construction company, accommodates its aging workforce through job adaptation and medical supervision. This involves a company doctor examining older workers and offering advice on the appropriate workloads for employees. Some of the job adaptations include: switching to supervisory positions; mentoring of younger workers, with the younger workers carrying out the more strenuous tasks; and the adjustment of the pace of work.

Other examples of age related ergonomic adjustments include:

- At Gloucester Housing Association, a UK organization, a telephone signal amplifier attachment was provided with a 'hands-free car kit' to assist an older worker experiencing some loss of hearing. (Gloucester Housing Association is a non profit making organization that provides good quality, affordable homes for people who have a housing need in Gloucestershire and its surrounding counties).

Age Concern Hull, UK, provided additional heating in a room occupied by an older worker (Age Concern Hull is based in Hull, serves people above 50 years, and employs about 50 people staff plus over 300 volunteers. They are affiliated to Age Concern England, but operate independently from it, and are a registered charity).

Technology and Tools for an Aging Workforce

Technology is serving as an equalizer for people of all ages and people with disabilities, increasing opportunities for employment and independent living while reducing social isolation. Accessible technology provides workers with the ability to personalize their computing environment and adapt it to meet their specific needs, allowing employees of all ages and abilities to realize their full potential.

Hardware, software applications, websites and user interfaces must be both functionally usable and technically accessible for an aging workforce. Focusing on accessibility will enhance usability and improve the computing and Web experience for users of all ages. Employers need to implement training programs in accessible technology and establish policies to ensure that accessibility is a criterion in the selection and procurement of information technology.

One of the primary misperceptions of many employers is that older workers have more difficulty learning and adapting to new technologies. However, a number of research studies have demonstrated that age alone is not directly linked to the adoption of computer use in the work environment.[7] For example, a recent case study involving mature workers at the UK retailer Tesco found that, while not all older workers were initially comfortable using new technologies, many quickly adapted to it. Motivation was cited as one of the primary drivers for adopting new technologies. As one manager stated, the mature workers were the ones "studying the literature, making use of telephone help-lines and suffering the restless nights making sure they could do the job."[8]

However, organizations should be cognizant of two issues related to the use of technology by mature workers: First, organizations need to consider the accessibility requirements of older workers. As individuals age, it may become more difficult to decipher smaller typefaces on a screen, understand the audio portion of a streaming video, or control the hand motions necessary to use a computer mouse or similar devices requiring precise movements. When designing systems, companies need to address the needs of potential user groups and provide alternative mechanisms for accessing, displaying and manipulating Web-pages and other applications. Furthermore, organizations need to evaluate the strategies associated with rolling out and training older workers on new applications. Organizations should consider building a cadre of influence leaders to demonstrate to older workers that they are capable of learning the new technologies, and build in ample practice opportunities to build comfort and confidence among individuals who have less experience in using the technology.[9]

The Digital Workplace and the Aging Workforce[10]

As the world is increasingly changing into an information-dependent society, technology has rapidly become a common fixture in the workplace. More and more occupations are becoming information-based, opening new employment opportunities for many people, including the aging workforce.

Workplace computing has expanded to include a variety of devices, applications and occupations. Use goes beyond the desktop to the production shop floor, the construction site, airport terminals and other occupations where workers need to be able to access and enter information. Fueling this is the growth in connectivity as evidenced by the proliferation of mobile devices such as personal digital assistants, wireless phones and public Wi-Fi Internet access. These workplace computing and Internet users, or information workers, are active participants in the process of business information flow. Specific occupations range from air traffic controllers and financial analysts to front-line workers such as factory employees, field service representatives, rental car agents and delivery people who use wireless reporting and tracking devices.

By making a commitment to workforce computing accessibility, companies can reap the benefit of productivity gains and the value of retaining knowledgeable workers. Accessibility is about removing barriers and providing access, making products and services available to, and usable by, everyone. A more accessible environment benefits every worker, including those with disabilities. To be accessible, technology must be flexible enough to meet the needs and preferences of a diverse cross-section of people with varied experience and abilities. Fortunately, many of the physiological changes associated with aging can easily be accommodated with current computers and computing platforms. When considering technological solutions to accommodate an aging workforce, employers should first consider the accessibility features that may already be available (but not yet activated) in their existing hardware and software, as well as third-party add-on assistive technology products.

Accessibility features are options in a product that allow older worker-users to adjust the product settings to accommodate their individual accessibility needs. Such usage and personalization benefit all users by offering increased usability, productivity, efficiency and comfort. Specific features can be accessibility to a range of vision, hearing, mobility, language and learning needs. Examples of accessibility features include those that allow a user to increase font size, change font settings or choose different colors for their computer screen. Other examples are the option for users to receive announcements from their computer through sound notifications, such as when new e-mail messages arrive, or visual notifications, such as a dialog box that appears, notifying users of new e-mail messages. While these features are included in commonly used technology and computer systems, they are not obvious to all users.

Numerous accessibility features built into standard computer operating systems can help people with mild age-related *vision impairments* use their computers and computing devices more comfortably and effectively. Accessibility solutions for visual impairments include simple user adjustments to the computer display, such as enlarging fonts and customizing color displays, and the use of screen-magnification aids.

Accessibility features built into standard computer operating systems are useful to people with *impaired mobility,* and include keyboard filters that help compensate for erratic motion, tremors, slow response time and similar conditions. One such example is Microsoft StickyKeys, which allow the user to enter key combinations sequentially without having to hold one key down while depressing a second. Users can adjust mouse properties such as button configuration, double-click speed, pointer and cursor size, and how quickly the mouse pointer responds to movements of the mouse. Computer users can also increase the size of screen elements to provide a larger mouse target, which can benefit people who have impairments related to fine-motor skills.

Accessibility features for people with *hearing loss* include settings that allow the users to change sound notification to visual notification and to control volume. Certain computing options allow users to receive visual warnings and text captions rather than audible messages to inform them of system events.

Assistive technology products are those that are designed to specifically accommodate an individual's disability (or multiple disabilities). Assistive technology products (also known as accessibility aids) are developed to work with a computer's operating system and software. Assistive technology can be anything from a different type of pointing device that takes the place of a mouse to a system equipped with a Braille display and screen reader. People with visual impairments can now have instant access to vast quantities of online information and "read" e-mail instantly without having to wait for documents to be converted to Braille or audiotape. Those with limited dexterity can use choice recognition software to perform work-related tasks such as writing documents and creating presentations and business analyses.

More than 100 companies offer hardware devices, accessories, aids and software applications that fall under the umbrella of assistive technology. These alternative input products include speech recognition systems, alternative keyboards, electronic pointing devices, sip-and-puff systems, wands, sticks, joysticks, trackballs and touch screens; and alternative output systems such as speech synthesizers, Braille embossers and displays, and screen readers.

In summary, accessible technology encompasses three elements: a) accessibility features, b) assistive technology products and c) compatibility among the operating system, software and assistive technology products. The compatibility of the operating system is a critical component of accessible technology, ensuring that product innovation in mainstream products does not prevent users of varying physical capabilities from using the peripherals and interfaces that they rely on for their livelihoods.

The Need to Establish Electronic Workplace Platforms Among an Aging Workforce

As the workforce ages, retirees take with them unique knowledge such as how products are developed, who suppliers are, where important records are kept, and how software products are applied to particular projects. It is essential to have workplace platforms that display the following features:[11]

- *Documented expertise – which employees know which subjects*

  While most firms have some sort of telephone directory of employees, their catalogs of employee traits are almost always limited to reporting structure and contact information. Employee directories offer no clues as to what each employee's area of expertise or specialization is, what their background is, or whether they are in the office at any given time. In contrast, the Blue Pages component of IBM's 'w3' intranet provides employee profiles that are populated with each worker's biographical information, resume, certifications, areas of expertise, and whether they are online for a quick instant messaging query.

- *Offering of an infrastructure to help employees help themselves*
  In many enterprises, email or poorly maintained internal websites are workers' only resources for finding the information they need to do their jobs. But at IBM, more than 250 information brokers nominate content and send links of relevant information for specific topics into an enterprise-wide taxonomy, such as financial services, procurement, or customer relationship management (CRM). The result is that enterprise marketing representatives in the field can search for terms like 'SAP' and 'CRM' and find thousands of documents, online resources, and even employees who have profiled their involvement in SAP's CRM.

- *Creating an electronic environment for meeting and sharing*
  Even in organizations where geographically dispersed workers need to collaborate frequently, most meetings are still held via conference call or in person, and email is the primary mechanism of electronic information sharing. In contrast, IBM's 'w3' intranet provides online team workspaces and electronic meeting environments that enable inexpensive, real-time collaboration – and keep a public record of ideas, conversations, and shared documents. IBM has also used 'w3' to run global online events, including a threaded discussion for 30,000 managers to engage in a time-limited discussion about management issues.

- *Institutionalized processes for high-skill positions*
  Although many firms are concerned about losing employees with unique expertise in areas like procurement, sourcing, hardware repair, and legacy system maintenance, few require important process documents like RFPs (requests for proposals)

and repair orders to be logged. Within the IBM 'w3' intranet, searchers can find the title and specialty of these types of contract negotiations. And the procurement processes have been altered to ensure that RFPs are entered into a system, making them subsequently retrievable.

Enterprises that are concerned about the impact of departing expertise over the next decade should evaluate progress in four major workplace areas to help preserve enterprise memory:[12]

(1) Establish a platform for collaboration

Most firms are still in the experimentation stage with collaboration tools, spawning a gaggle of vendor point solutions for team collaboration, Web conferencing, and instant messaging. The most sophisticated companies, such as IBM, will forge a firm-wide collaboration strategy. This not only enables corporate memory retention, but it also allows firms to save money by consolidating redundant infrastructure and retiring the tools that run on it. As an intermediate step, companies should use portal technology for lightweight publishing, community portal sites, and integration of certain tools as portlets.

(2) Organize critical content so that it is retrievable online

As firms inventory their software assets en route to an enterprise collaboration strategy, they may include the use of an enterprise content management (ECM) framework to capture and organize documents, Web content, email, or other records. Firms must also evaluate whether the search tools of either the collaboration platform or the ECM framework are adequate as they begin to replace existing information silos and previous failed search implementations. They should decide whether the enterprise benefits from centrally managed/distributed maintenance of topic categories, as in the IBM w3 environment. As an intermediate step, firms should build on index across both ECM and legacy sources with a single set of retrieval algorithms.

(3) Integrate expertise location into directories and jobs

From the employee perspective, expertise locators within the intranet help them to find out who knows what, and even allow them to ask questions. But to make sure that experts are willing to be found, supervisors should integrate the update of information into workers' job requirements and ensure that it is up-to-date at review time. They should then mandate populating a complete profile as part of the new hire process.

(4) Document and automate critical business processes

It is important to settle on a business process management (BPM) strategy, starting first with high-cost manual processes, such as paper-based records management and forms-based processes. BPM technologies use rules engines to capture key policies in an application-independent, human readable form, and they include tools that allow those policies to be maintained by practitioners, not by IT. To capture process knowledge, companies should make sure that new, automated processes output a record of key transactions, and they should add documentation of these new processes to the ECM repository.

Key Pointers of Chapter 8

- The work environments and physical tools of most enterprises are not customized to meet the changing needs of an aging workforce. It is important that a new set of work environment models are adopted as soon as possible, in view of the aging workforce.

- With physical changes in workers' muscles, bones, cardiovascular, respiratory, hearing, skin, sensory and hearing processes, it is crucial to recognize how such changes impact on the work environment, and what employers and workers respectively need to do about it for future maintenance and increase in productivity and creativity.

- Guidelines for the design and development of new ergonomic models for an aging workforce, based on research projects such as RESPECT, as well as leading company examples, are valuable for devising customized approaches, such as ergonomic-adjusted short breaks, reduction of working time, and redesigned shift systems.

- Seven work environment action fields have been identified, i.e. leadership actions, use of expert knowledge, working time actions, recruitment policies, project work, human resources development, and public relations. It shows that each V-field is also interrelated with all of the other fields.

- Technology and tools for an aging workforce should especially include the digital workplace, with focus on accessibility, assistive products, workplace platforms, and measures to preserve enterprise memory through integrated workplace expertise location processes.

9 The Fifth V-Field: Human Resources Management (HRM) Approaches for Managing the Aging Workforce

Key Issues of this Chapter

- The challenges and changing role of HRM concerning an aging workforce
- HRM strategies and work models for an aging workforce
- Key HRM action fields for an aging workforce
- Critical perspectives and steps for successful HRM programs

The Challenges and Changing Role of HRM Concerning an Aging Workforce

Across especially the developed world, today's enterprises are encountering the reality of an aging workforce and changing workforce demographics for their HRM departments and activities. Not only are many organizations losing valuable workers (and invaluable organizational knowledge) through attrition and retirements, but they are also challenged to understand and utilize the particular motivations, career aspirations, and values that their older workers who remain in the workforce bring, in order to sustain their continued involvement and participation. Furthermore, intergenerational dynamics and conflicts in the workplace provide a challenging context and set of problems for human resource professionals and their practices.

Human resources departments and their functions, as we know them today, are not well aligned with the profiles and values of many individuals within this century's workforce. Hierarchical structures, rigid job designs, unilateral employment relationships, and cascading decision-making are at odds with the idealistic values of the baby-boomer cohort and the greater independence of cohorts to follow. Our business organizations and employment policies face the significant challenge to adapt to the needs and values of the new workforce.

The major HRM challenge of the 21st century is how to effectively use and retain the skills and capabilities of an aging workforce. This will require new and more flexible approaches to the "deal" between employers and employees, and new and more "democratic" forms of corporate organizations. Most importantly, it involves new assumptions about work and workers.[1] In a fundamental sense, reshaping the relationship between employees and employers is critically important. Today's workforce already experiences alarmingly low levels of engagement in work. *Improving job involvement – finding ways to encourage individuals to invest more psychic and mental energy in work – is the single most powerful lever that most corporations have to improve productivity.*[2] After decades of downsizing, rightsizing, and re-engineering, most corporations have virtually exhausted their ability to squeeze increased productivity out of the system through top-down pressure. The opportunity today is to raise our engagement with work – to tap appropriately into the productivity, creativity, and passion of the aging workforce. Creating higher engagement levels in an aging workforce is about recognizing individual strengths, needs, preferences, and values. Companies need to shift the human resource paradigm from a focus on "equality" played out by treating everyone the same, to "fair, but customized", reflecting different arrangements suited to individual needs and preferences of an aging workforce.

While the characteristics of the aging workforce are changing, so too are significant advances in technology driving the way our enterprises and HRM departments operate. These advances will both reinforce and enable the desires of individual workers, allowing greater personal flexibility, autonomy and participation and, as a result, increased corporate productivity and creativity.

Low engagement levels demonstrate that for most aging employees the current "employment deal" isn't working well. *Our research shows that employers place too much emphasis on traditional compensation and benefits and the tangible elements of the employment relationship, and too little emphasis on the heart of the required new deal – the human relationships, values, and work design itself, and what the integrated experience of all these factors does for the heart and soul of the aging employee.*

Employers chronically underestimate the fundamental importance to aging employees of stimulating, meaningful work, and very few employers have a realistic sense of how many employees feel "dead-ended" and why. In fact, all employees place extremely high value on their work and the workplace. When a nationwide survey had employees state their relative preference for ten basic elements of the employment deal, the security items – comprehensive benefits packages and comprehensive retirement packages – topped the list. But the next three items were all about work and workplace: work that enables me to learn, grow and try new things; a workplace that is enjoyable; and work that is personally stimulating. The most innovative, accomplished, and already-engaged employees value work and the workplace the highest, often above the security items.[3]

A survey of human resources directors by IBM in 2005 concluded: "When the baby-boomer generation retires, many companies will find out too late that a career's worth of experience has walked out the door, leaving insufficient talent to fill the void."[4]

One of the major reasons that most companies – and especially their HRM departments – are not doing anything yet about the aging workforce, is that the implications of the demographic treads are beyond their mental horizons. Their mindsets are still firmly rooted in traditional retirement practices, established compensation and benefit packages, fixed career policies, and traditional views of the meaning of work and behavior of older employees.

Managing human resources in a period of demographic decline and increasing life expectancy is one of the major challenges companies face today – new HR strategies, action fields and programs have become urgently necessary. Some companies have started to realize this, as indicated in the following box.[5]

How Some Companies are Changing Human Resources Management

Deutsche Bank recently decided to review its human resources policy because of its need to downsize. As a German bank, it had a long tradition of the apprenticeship system, where young people learn from older experienced workers. The age diversity approach is about older and younger employees benefiting from each other. It promotes exchange of knowledge and working together in age-diverse teams.

As the Thales Group grew, valuable senior managers were becoming redundant due to reorganization. The company did not want to lose them, yet their capabilities did not fit available jobs. A new business unit was needed to channel valuable capabilities into developing (new) company projects and future job-creation. Thus, the unit Missions & Conseil was created, providing a solution to this internal mobility problem and expanding to become much more than a career management system – in fact a driver for desired change within the group.

Various Finnish companies were motivated by national concerns for a high quality of life at work and life in general. Their experience revealed that many positive aspects of aging are relatively unknown and therefore unappreciated. Older people may suffer from declining short-term memory and a slower pace but, in the right work environment and with a flexible workload, older workers can maintain high productivity. Older workers possess a legion of strengths including good cumulative long-term memory, long working experience, good ability to evaluate issues and problems. These represent not only valuable assets for employers but also strong arguments against age discrimination. The Finnish Dahlbo company's HRM project serves as a good example regarding economic benefits. According to company research, the modest annual investment in a 'promote and maintain work ability' (PMWA) program paid back tenfold. The benefits included improved productivity and reduction of sick leave, work disability, and pension costs.

Whatever the initial reasons for implementing the above-mentioned programs, companies found themselves rethinking their most valuable asset: human capital. The company case examples show that programs initially developed for older workers were beneficial for the company as a whole. *Age management led not only to better human resources management, but also to better business management, and ultimately to better business performance.*

The changing role of the HRM function concerning an aging workforce is especially on two levels, viz:

- Shifting from rigid, traditional practices to flexible, dynamic practices that have a multi-dimensional view of an aging workforce, and not a one-dimensional one (see Figure 9.1).

- A significant change from an outward-looking, competitive mindset for required talent to a more inward, knowledge-retaining, age-ergonomic adjusted workplace, with flexible work, compensation and health arrangements.

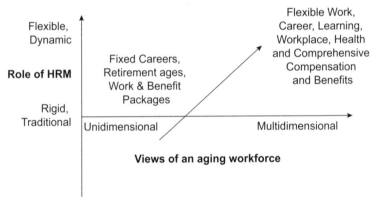

Figure 9.1
A flexible, dynamic role for HRM concerning an aging workforce

Figure 9.1 indicates the HRM role as viewing demographic change as a great opportunity for the enterprise. With the external competition for talent and skills becoming intense and costly, HRM is forced to look internally to identify, nurture, develop, and reward their aging workforce with flexible and dynamic approaches, arrangements, and tools. The next section discusses such HRM strategies and work models for an aging workforce.

HRM Strategies and Work Models for an Aging Workforce

Table 9.1 illustrates key human resources problems, strategy focus areas, and appropriate new work models for an aging workforce.

The key HRM Challenges in terms of organizational levels are indicated in Table 9.2.

From Tables 9.1 and 9.2 it can be seen that it is necessary to be clear about the particular strategy foci and work models to adopt in order to address the key aging workforce challenges. Goldberg also suggests a number of work models that can be adopted for an aging workforce:[6]

Table 9.1

Key HRM challenges, strategy foci, and new work models

Key HRM challenge	Strategy focus	New work model
Career policy *Recruitment practice* *Retention practice*	Corporate culture Retention, flexible work Staff relationships	Extended/variation careers Working options Internal PR & communication
Leadership & managerial mindsets	Age & aging Aging value-added Nurturing & guiding	Reorientation seminars Contract & consulting work Mentoring
Staff development *Knowledge management* *Learning & training* *Work practices*	Staff operation & rotation KM retention & transfer Organizational learning Phased work	Variable team functions Knowledge identification, capture & sharing Org. learning measures Value chain phased activity
Individual health *Health programs*	Mental health Physical health Emotional health & organizational energy	Meaningful work Physical exercising Positive energy applications
Work environment *Physical tools*	Age ergonomics Work organization Technology platforms	Workplace reorganization Flexible work routines Digital work activities Telecommuting
Compensation & benefits	Comprehensive & meaningful benefits	Financial & non-financial rewards; work/life harmony

Table 9.2

Key HRM challenges and organizational levels

Organizational level	Key HRM challenges
Leadership level *(e.g. Board of Directors)*	Mindsets Public Relations (PR)
Management level	Mentoring Recruitment policy Staff development Change of company culture Knowledge Management Attitudes
Process level	Working time Project work Work arrangements (age-ergonomics)
Individual level	Speed performances Motivation Attitude Health

(1) Full-time permanent work with flexibility

The most common flexible arrangements for full-time workers are flexitime (people decide to start their day at a time of their choosing between 8:00am and 10:00am and leave eight hours later) or compression (these arrangements tend to involve either working less days every two weeks with shorter lunch hours or four 10-hour days a week with normal lunch hours).

(2) Part-time permanent work

These jobs are for less than 40 hours a week. They may call for two or three full-time days, five half-time days, or any other combination, but they are not limited in duration. Included in this category is the somewhat new concept of shared jobs, a development that was pushed by new mothers who wanted to reduce their time at work for a few years without exiting the workforce.

(3) Full-time and part-time temporary work

Although most of these jobs are in the service industry, particularly in sales, about 20 percent of these workers are ranked as professionals. Today, the majority of people in these jobs are under 35; in the future, older workers are likely to make up the largest group in this category. A significant development in this area is the use of former employees who temporarily return to the organizations from which they have retired. A pioneer in this area is Travelers Corporation, which set up such a service for retired workers some two decades ago and has had such success with it that other companies have adopted similar programs. This approach is extremely beneficial to an organization because former employees understand the organization's culture and know the ways things work.

(4) Contract or consulting work

Organizations like these arrangements because they allow them to add workers temporarily for specific projects while providing more stability than would be the case with temporary workers from agencies. This is particularly important when companies need to add people to teams that are set up to handle large short-term projects. In these situations, companies often entice retired workers to return for the life of the project because they understand the corporate culture, making things run far more smoothly.

(5) Telecommuting

The arrangements to work preliminary from home, which are made possible by technology, are still taking shape, but it has become clear that they offer advantages and disadvantages. New "rules of the road", especially performance measurement and managerial training, will have to be developed to ensure that telecommuters are successful. In addition, for some older employees, at-home work can make life easier if money is the major reason for returning to work. Working at home, however, does not bring the social interaction that makes work so attractive to other older workers.

(6) On-call work

The terms of on-call work often involve a guaranteed minimum number of hours. Organizations that must be fully staffed at all times in certain areas, such as hospitals, tend to make these arrangements. For the organization, it ensures that back-up personnel is available at relatively low cost whenever needed. For workers, it eliminates some of the uncertainty involved in finding temporary work. Since on-call work usually involves varying shifts, it is ideal for older workers who have few specific demands on their time. The following box illustrates how ASDA attracts older workers on a part-time and on-call basis.[7]

How ASDA Attracts Older Workers on a Part-Time and On-Call Basis

ASDA, the UK's largest retailer, has recognized the value of attracting mature workers on a part-time basis. The company has over 20,000 employees who are over 50 years old, representing 19 percent of its workforce. ASDA conducts over-50 workshops at local job recruitment centers in the UK for anyone interested in continuing to work, not just those interested in working for ASDA. They also provide a number of flexible arrangements and benefits targeted toward older workers, such as "Benidorm leave" (three months unpaid leave between January and March) and "Grandparent leave" (a week unpaid leave after the birth of a grandchild). Recently, the company opened a store in the UK where 40 percent of the associates were over age 50. ASDA has found this focus on flexible arrangements for aging workers provided a number of organizational benefits, especially in periods of high-density customer support, such as key festival periods. Stores with a higher proportion of older workers have absenteeism rates less than a third of ASDA'S average rate. Also, in March 2003, ASDA was selected as 1 of Britain's top 10 companies to work for, and the UK's best company for flexible working.

(7) Phased retirement

Under phased retirement, older employees work out a plan for withdrawing from the company. They reduce the number of days they work each week by, say, a day the first three months, then two days for the next three months, and so on until they reach full retirement. This benefits the organization because it allows for a transfer of the expertise and institutional knowledge of the retiring worker to the person who will eventually take over the job. Scripps Health is an example of a company practicing this, as indicated in the following box.[8]

Phased-Retirement Plans at Scripps Health

Scripps Healths, a San Diego-based (U.S.) health-care provider estimates that it will have to replace 40 percent of its 10,000 employees within the next five years. And in certain departments, such as imaging and outpatient diagnostics, that figure is closer to 70 percent.

To encourage older workers to stay on past retirement age, Scripps is doing everything from restructuring jobs to offering phased-retirement plans. In October 2004, for example, the company created the role of "clinical mentor," which allows experienced nurses to forgo some of the more physically demanding aspects of their jobs, such as moving and lifting patients, in favor of acting as expert resources to those with less experience. It also permits workers with 10 or more years of experience to reduce their work hours while retaining full benefits. And Scripps modified its retirement-plan rules in the spring of 2004 to let some older employees tap funds to supplement reduced work schedules. So far, the steps seem to be paying off. More than 16 percent of its 10,400 employees are over the age of 55.

And keeping some workers from full retirement has an immediate benefit by raising turnover. It costs Scripps as much as $50,000 to replace a nurse. Another significant expense in this labor-challenged sector is per diem (contract) staff. Scripps's efforts to retain its own employees have allowed it to cut its per diem expenses by one-third, saving about $10 million.

(8) Job-sharing

A company facing the loss of a large number of older workers can offer the opportunity for them to stay on half-time, sharing their jobs with other older workers who choose to work when retired, but also prefer a less hectic schedule. A department with six people, four of whom are ready for retirement, could end up having to hire only two new people if two can be persuaded to job-share. The result would be a far smoother transition.

(9) Bridge employment

In bridge employment, an older worker is often given special assignments, such as serving on a disaster recovery project or representing the company in a community project. It also includes assignments that would disrupt younger workers' lives. For example, Whirlpool Corporation finds it is less expensive to hire retired workers for short-term assignments abroad than to relocate full-time workers. Quaker Oats has tapped retirees for a project in Shanghai. GE also has tested this approach and plans to expand it.

(10) Mentoring

When organizations are concerned about maintaining their institutional history and values, and even some older skills and techniques, they often turn to older workers, who can answer such questions as: Why were certain decisions about processes made? Why don't we do business with company X (and who has to leave before we can try to get in the door again)? This is information that does not get captured in memos or expert systems; it is the stuff of history, stored in memory, recounted as conversation. One of the ways companies can capture this knowledge is to ask older workers to become mentors, training younger employees so that the expertise and experience they have acquired over long years are passed on rather than lost.

The following box indicates three companies named by the American Association of Retired Persons (AARP) as best-practice companies for flexible work options for workers over the age of 50.[9]

Three Companies Recognized for Flexible Work Options for Older Workers by the 2004 "AARP Best Employers for Workers Over 50" Awards Program

Outside Work Options: The Principal Financial Group, Des Moines, IA, USA

The Principal Financial Group reported two programs that provide temporary transfer opportunities for managers and other senior-level employees so that they can work at the local offices of charities, the United Way, and in international assignments.

While posts at the United Way and charities are for 2 to 3 months, the international assignments are for 2 to 3 years. Unlike management training programs that aim to cycle newer employees through a broad range of positions, these programs target more experienced and oftentimes older workers. They receive job and transfer opportunities that would not otherwise be available to them. The posts in charities also serve to promote the company.

Job Mobility for Older Workers: Deere & Company, Moline, IL, USA

In 2004, Deere & Company launched "a self-nomination process for job openings for career movement." The company has "many team and special assignments that are provided for development, along with task forces, presentations and steering committees." As part of the annual performance review process, managers are encouraged to seek opportunities for job movement with employees. The advantage is that mature workers receive opportunities for mobility and skill-building that are institutionalized in the company that may be uncommon in other organizations.

Job Mobility: The MITRE Corporation, Bedford, MA/McLean, VA, USA

The MITRE Corporation allows employees to "change jobs without changing employers." This initiative is designed to encourage internal transfers and encourages managers to offer 8 to 10 % of staff an opportunity to transfer to a new internal job each year. While not explicitly aimed at mature workers, this policy allows workers of all ages opportunities to move laterally and to gain broader experiences. Such practices can lead to higher job satisfaction, greater employee commitment, and a broader knowledge base. However, there is a risk. When employees are transferred to new roles too often it could reduce their ability to complete longer-term projects efficiently.

Key HRM Action Fields for an Aging Workforce

From the above-mentioned HRM strategy foci and related new work model options, four key HRM action fields for an aging workforce emerge. These are highlighted in this section: knowledge retention and transfer; flexible learning and training; comprehensive compensation and benefits; and extended/variation careers. HRM is an integrated issue, however, and the obvious reason why other action fields such as health, work environment, and mindset change are not discussed here, is because they are outlined in depth in other chapters of this book.

HRM's Role in Knowledge Retention and Transfer

While knowledge management is a much wider, systemic concept – as described in Chapter 6 – the focus here is on knowledge retention and transfer of an aging workforce due to the critical dangers of 'lost knowledge' from an imminent wave of retirees. HRM should address four major challenges to retain and transfer knowledge in the enterprise:[10]

a) What is our organization's current skill and knowledge base, and how will it need to change, given our strategy?

b) How do we do replacement planning for key employees? And how do we make certain their successors have been adequately prepared to fill those critical positions?

c) Does our culture support behaviors needed for ongoing knowledge retention and transfer?

d) How can we encourage highly skilled older employees to stay longer?

HRM needs an integrated set of human resource capabilities to address these issues, viz:

- Organizational skill bases and systems for evaluating them
- Succession planning processes
- Developing a 'retention and transfer' culture
- Policies and practices to retain older workers.

These four human resource capabilities are briefly outlined here:

(1) Systems for evaluating organizational skills bases

No enterprise can systematically evaluate current 'lost knowledge' threats, or its future needs for knowledge development, without a detailed inventory of current capabilities. Knowing what skills the enterprise's workforce has, where they are located geographically, who would possibly move/depart, and how to act to retain these skills, is especially critical today. Comprehensive and practical processes that monitor existing capabilities will improve the quality of management decisions about organization-wide skill development and, at the same time, reduce the likelihood that your best people are the ones laid off. *Although technology can certainly be helpful, monitoring your skill base must be a human-centered process because it takes experienced managers to interpret the complex mix of skills and knowledge each employee has and to build trust in how the process is being used.*

(2) Succession planning processes

Once HRM have identified those employees with the most critical knowledge or hard-to-replace skills, they need a way to allocate resources in developing and retaining these people, but also appropriate succession planning and career development processes, which should be integrated into a long-term succession management system. Historically, most organizations have limited succession planning to leadership roles, but managers increasingly recognize the need to extend the practice in the organization to cover other essential professional and managerial roles. The increased reliability on complex technical, scientific, and professional knowledge makes succession planning essential for a much broader set of positions in many organizations.

Succession Planning at Siemens[11]

Siemens, Europe's largest electronics and electrical engineering firm, has a global personnel development process that requires an annual dialogue between managers and their employees. Part of the conversation is intended to clarify expectations around the employee's next career move from his or her current position. The manager and employee are expected to develop a mutually agreeable answer to this question. If the next career move is expected to occur in less than a year (either within Siemens or leaving the firm), then there is a standard process similar to a succession plan that they must follow to find a replacement and begin the process of transferring knowledge.

Succession planning is important to expose emerging gaps in leadership, management, and other employees before they affect performance. This type of activity will also help to identify successors early enough to provide adequate time for knowledge transfer. While succession planning can help preempt knowledge loss for the organization, career development processes may be one of the most effective retention tools for key employees. Career development processes can increase retention in tight labor markets by signaling to individuals that the organization is interested in their personal development. *Keeping highly skilled employees challenged and focused on realistic future opportunities with the organization is an important source of commitment that is needed to support long-term knowledge-sharing behaviors.*

(3) Developing a 'retention and transfer' culture

Retaining employees can assist in retaining critical knowledge, but employee retention and knowledge retention are not the same thing. Low turnover, for example, does not mean that knowledge is necessarily being shared and retained in critical areas. An effective retention and transfer culture consists of values, norms, and practices that encourage high-performing and highly skilled employees to stay.

Such an ideal culture would also encourage knowledge retention by rewarding behaviors such as mentoring, coaching, and information sharing. Thus, "retention culture" includes both how a culture influences who stays and who leaves an organization, as well as how it encourages behaviors related to knowledge transfer. These behaviors include a willingness to share, as well as regularly seeking out and reusing existing knowledge. Retention is just one of many dimensions along which an organization's culture can be assessed – others might include quality, agility, teamwork, and accountability. *The key elements that comprise a culture that values knowledge retention and transfer are: high levels of trust; support for individual development; and high levels of process/functional integration and collaboration.* These elements can only be developed and sustained if the enterprise's systems, processes, and practices – such as performance values and compensation systems – are aligned to support them.

(4) Policies and practices to retain older workers

The policies and practices an enterprise has in place to entice highly skilled older employees to keep working beyond retirement eligibility will be a key to minimizing the costs of lost knowledge.

DeLong suggests at least four actions that management can implement to retain older workers:[12]

- Align the enterprise's retirement benefits (e.g. pension) with its objectives for employee retention.

- Educate older workers about retirement planning.

- Publicize phased retirement as an option – as a formal or informal program.

- Diagnose and influence the enterprise's attitude towards older workers.

A major barrier to the success of these initiatives will be the enterprise's cultural attitude towards older workers – to retain them, they must feel that their experience and work contributions are valued by management.

The following box provides examples of companies that offer es-
teem-raising programs for older workers.[13]

Company Examples of Esteem-Raising Programs for Older Workers

Lufthansa, the German airline, recognized that many of its older workers were not participating in learning activities. An annual evaluation of its training showed that the company had not offered systematic training opportunities for older workers for more then 10 years. To address the learning needs of managers older than 45, the company started an initiative called the "Added Experience Program."

The objectives of this program are threefold: to transfer informal skills that have not been taught and that are necessary in the working environment, to create a dialogue among participants that facilitates the exchange of valuable experiences and enables managers to increase the size and scope of their personal networks, and to allow top management to learn about, and tap into, the know-how these older experienced managers brought to the table. The program lasts for one year and consists of a number of one-week modules. The participants stay in the same cohort throughout the year to build a level of trust that is needed to share lessons learned and good practices.

General Electric, at the dawn of the e-commerce era, matched 500 of its most older senior managers with junior employees to learn about the potential for Internet technologies. The "junior" mentors and the "seniors" were paired based on knowledge and personality traits, and then spent two to four hours per week together, discussing the 'ins and outs' of the World Wide Web. As a result of this process, the older senior executives gained new insights that were critical to moving their businesses into the Internet age, while the junior employees were able to gain access to a network of experienced older executives that, under normal circumstances, would be difficult to obtain.

Flexible Learning and Training[14]

Older workers, including many past the prevailing retirement age, want to keep working in a less time-consuming, less-pressured capacity so that they can pursue other interests. They want time for recreation and volunteerism, doing what their previous working lives did not allow. Naturally interested in reduced and flexible schedules, they show the highest preference for a flexible workplace and for experimentation, such as taking six months on, six months off.

The center of gravity of corporate learning and training should therefore shift today from the company as provider to the employee as consumer – with flexible and self-managed learning, training, best-practice sharing, community-of-practice orientation, and knowledge expansion. Progressive HRM should actively and systemically guide and influence these activities for coherence with the enterprise's objectives and requirements.

Types of flexible work are:

- *Flexible time*

  includes flexible hours and shifts (work schedules that permit flexible starting and quitting times within limits set by management) and compressed working weeks (for example, a forty-hour working week compressed into four ten-hour days instead of the usual five eight-hour days).

- *Reduced time*

  includes part-time and seasonal work, job sharing (regular, part-time work where people share responsibilities of one full-time, salaried position with benefits), reduced hours or days worked, and various less-than-full-time contract assignments.

- *Flexible place*

  includes telecommuting (working primarily from home), mobile work (such as a salesperson who works predominantly on the road), and other forms of off-site work.

Flexible work is not new, and most major companies already offer some combination of flexible time, reduced time, and flexible place. But there is a big difference between offering flexible arrangements to some workers and implementing flexiwork on a large scale that reaps real business benefits.

Flexible Work and Learning at Home Depot[15]

Home Depot uses several forms of flexible work arrangements, including flexible schedules and part-time work, to retain its many mid-career and mature workers, some of them workforce re-entrants, whose knowledge and experience translates into excellent customer service in their stores. This flexibility appeals to those who are "semi-retired" but keeping busy, and over half such employees have flexible schedules. The company also grants employees time to participate in community volunteer projects and offers flexible vacation schedules and leaves of absence for numerous personal reasons.

Several preconditions for the successful implementation of flexible learning and training initiatives have to be met:

- Always relate such initiatives to enterprise goals and objectives.

- Develop clear policy guidelines, and evaluation measures, for flexible learning and training initiatives.

- Integrate such initiatives into individual work schedules and performance objectives.

- Maintain cohesiveness – continuity and coherence – as flexible programs increase.

- Adequately communicate and publicize flexible learning and training initiatives in the enterprise.

- Ensure management commitment and consistency in these initiatives.

Comprehensive Compensation and Benefits

Until recently, employee compensation and benefits predominantly consisted of salaries, wages, commissions, bonuses, and standardized health and retirement benefits. With the increasing aging of the workforce, and increasing workforce mobility, diversity, virtual work practices, flatter organization structures, and employee consumerism, a range of new measures is becoming necessary. Competition for talent intensifies as labor markets

Table 9.3

Towards comprehensive aging-related compensation and benefits[16]

Element	From	To
Pay	Tenure based, mainly cash	Performance based, more equity
Pension	Defined benefit	Defined contribution, cash balance
Health benefits	Employer managed and provided	Co-funded and co-managed
Other benefits	Standard	Many choices, 'cafeteria'-style, customized
Recognition and reward	Formal, periodic	Formal and informal, immediate (on-the-spot)

tighten, and the most talented workers are the most sophisticated consumers, looking for the best-tailored employee deals. Costs spiral as the workforce ages, health-care costs march upward, government mandates increase, and employers face the added effort and cost of handling complicated benefits options and customizing employee deals.

To attract and retain talent in the future, enterprises must handle the variety of new employee needs, accommodate employee mobility, customize more employees' deals, and get all facets of the employment deal right (see Table 9.3). Most enterprises have taken significant steps in these directions: cafeteria-style benefits, portable defined-contribution pensions, and compensation plans with long-term components like stock grants. But there's much more work to be done as workforce composition changes and competition for skilled people intensifies.

Enterprises have to wisely accommodate, with assistance of their HRM, the making of their compensation and benefits for an aging workforce appropriately comprehensive and attractive, within the inevitably escalating costs of such extensions, i.e. without collapsing under untenable cost structures. Dychtwald et.al. indicate six major challenges in managing compensation and benefits for an aging workforce:[17]

- *Customization*: focusing on individual requirements and unique packaging

- *Segmentation*: crafting benefits around meaningful employee segments, in terms of their needs both on the job and at home

- *Overall combination and impacts*: focusing on the value and fit of the package, as a combination of benefits – financial, healthcare, family support, and persona interests

- *Integration*: simplify, streamline, and coordinate benefits into the "employee deal"

- *Fairness*: equitable practices across roles, functions, and responsibilities

- *Accessibility*: easy grasp, easy choices of combinations, and easy consumption of the benefits by employees

Extended/Variation Careers

The fourth key HRM action field concerning an aging workforce is the extension of careers after regular retirement, as well as greater options and variety in careers. In fact, the term 'career' is becoming obsolete, being replaced by a term such as 'talent application path', indicating a broader spectrum of application of talents – despite an individual's core profession or education platform.

Three broad categories of actions are suggested: the rejuvenation of talent application paths; recruitment of returning retirees; and attracting aging workers to strengthen managerial and leadership positions. Employees are ultimately responsible for their own talent development, meaningful work choices, and marketability, but HRM is responsible for assisting aging employees to perceive this, to understand it, and to make wise mutual decisions.

- *Rejuvenation of talent application paths*

  Most people wish to live interesting and meaningful lives, and to reinvent themselves and the value they bring to enterprises and society in general. Their talent applications (or 'careers') can be rejuvenated by measures such as fresh assignments, mentoring roles, variations in talent application, new training programs and sabbaticals.

- *Recruitment of returning retirees*

  Many people, not only retirees but also those that have been retrenched, returning after maternity or other job experiments, can be productively recruited by HRM. The measures to be implemented consist of data bases resulting from inventories and audits of such people, nurturing of relationships, monitoring of intentions and objectives, targeted recruiting drives, and appropriate re-introduction into the workforce.

- *Attracting aging workers to strengthen management and leadership*

  In a knowledge-networked innovation economy the need for managers and leaders has become immense, and the aging workforce-related demographic trends point to an imminent crisis for many enterprises. Measures that can be implemented are: delay retirement of selected leaders, bring back retirees as interim managers or leaders, utilize retirees as coaches and mentors, and get retirees to assist in special projects. At the same time, it is important to intensify efforts in the existing leadership development process and to facilitate the co-existence of multiple generations in management and leadership.

Critical Perspectives and Steps for Successful HRM Programs

The concepts of "work", "age", and "retirement" have never been more ambiguous. More and more people will define themselves as the "working retired" in the future, and it is critical for HRM in enterprises to have the right perspectives concerning the needs, attitudes, lifestyles, meaningful work in an innovation economy, and expectations of compensation and benefits of an aging workforce. It is not a question of choice for HRM but a forceful reality that will be impacting on enterprises' competitiveness in the future.

HRM must first have the right perspective of what role they want older workers to play in their organization. This means, in part, clarifying the strategic impacts an aging workforce will have on the firm's workforce and leadership development. When trying to influence older worker retention, managers also must pay more attention to the behaviors that their organization's culture is condoning. One way to do this is to probe for mature workers' real perceptions of how the organization values them. An important lesson in this research is the folly of treating all older workers the same. *Indeed, stereotypes make us much less likely to notice the actual qualities and attributes that are most likely to determine an individual's real contribution.*

HRM should also benefit from examining their perspectives about the costs of retaining older workers. Important questions include: Are the costs of lost experience and knowledge being factored in? And what are the costs of expanding opportunities for older workers? HRM should anticipate – but not assume – changes in the sources of motivation for workers in their sixties. As studies have shown, the motivations for work do not change for everyone in the same way. *For some, the drive for economic gain never disappears, but for many others economic motives fall behind the need to accomplish something meaningful in their early sixties.*[18] One of the best ways to accommodate these changes is to design and implement creative ways to structure work and benefits for an increasingly aging workforce.

Another critical perspective for HRM to have is a sound sense and understanding of the factors encouraging retirement, i.e. limiting the adoption of a new HRM paradigm in the enterprise. Table 9.4 indicates a framework of factors encouraging retirement in the light of factors encouraging work.[19]

A number of critical steps for HRM to take in order to ensure that they will be prepared to successfully implement HR programs and deal with the challenges of an aging workforce are:

- *Conduct careful analyses of the demographics of the enterprise's workforce and the organization's future needs in view of competitive productivity and innovation challenges.*

- *Institute a company-wide policy of conducting regular interviews with crucial employees when they reach certain ages, e.g. 50, 55 and 60. Be careful to portray this as a way of determining reten-*

Table 9.4

Perspectives on factors encouraging respectively work and retirement

Factors encouraging work	Factors encouraging retirement
• Aging boomers want to apply talents longer • Employers recognize skills shortage and the need for older workers • Government needs to extend employment to reduce drain on the social security system	• Organizational cultures drive older workers out • Older workers seen as more costly • Enterprises do not provide the flexibility older workers need • Opportunities for older workers limited • Older workers' motivation for work changes • Older workers' misperceptions about financial needs

tion of valuable knowledge and talents, succession planning, and devising arrangements that could keep workers longer active in applying their talents, to mutual benefit of themselves and the enterprise.

- *Develop economically feasible and psychologically beneficial strategies for partial and extended retirement. The costs and benefits of the various arrangements discussed earlier in the chapter, ranging from job-sharing to phased retirement to an internal "temp" agency, need to be calculated so a set of choices can be offered to employees.*

- *Work with those who are in charge of retirement plans to ensure that when the time comes that the retention of older workers is necessary, those who want to work after a certain age are not penalized for it. Penalties for working after a certain age that were enacted when the company was looking for ways to encourage retirement need to be changed in time to help retain members of the baby-boom generation when the inevitable shortfall of trained workers occurs.*

- *For each of the key HRM areas, develop a clear strategy focus with particular new work models aimed at the aging workforce. Ensure that these are linked to each particular organizational level.*

- *Implement an integrated, coordinated HRM policy and strategies, including all HRM action fields.*

Key Pointers of Chapter 9

- HRM are facing critical challenges in mindsets, strategies, work models, action fields, and HR programs in dealing with an aging workforce.

- The changing role of HRM is evident especially on two levels, viz. a shift to flexible, dynamic practices based on a multi-dimensional view of an aging workforce; and a shift towards a more inward, knowledge-retaining, age-ergonomic adjusted workplace with flexible work, compensation, and health arrangements.

- Appropriate HRM strategy foci and new work models need to be identified and activated for each of the key HRM challenges, as indicated in this chapter.

- Four key HRM action fields were identified with accompanying guidelines, viz. knowledge retention and transfer; flexible learning and training; comprehensive compensation and benefits; and extended/variation careers.

- Critical perspectives for successful HRM programs for an aging workforce are a positive and knowledgeable sense of the nature, needs, attitudes, and expectations of older workers, the role they can play in the enterprise, the costs of retaining older workers, and the factors encouraging respectively retirement and work.

- Critical steps for HRM to successfully implement HR programs for the aging workforce are recommended.

PART IV

Putting It All Together

10 The 5V-Scorecard for Measuring the Performance of an Aging Workforce

Key Issues of this Chapter

- What overall performance of an aging workforce should be measured?
- The integrated 5V-Scorecard as a holistic measurement tool of the value-added of an aging workforce
- Combining implementation tools and measurement tools in managing the aging workforce
- The dynamics of utilizing the 5V-Scorecard

What Overall Performance of an Aging Workforce Should be Measured?

As indicated in Chapter 4, the two key value-adding dimensions of any workforce are increased productivity and increased creativity: productivity is predominantly an efficiency mechanism and measurement, concerned with either greater output for same input, or same output for less input, or ideally both. Existing managerial mindsets mainly consider the aging workforce as necessarily declining in productivity as aging progresses, and they expect that workforce creativity – for innovation and development of new product propositions – will decrease due to aging.

The five major enterprise action fields (5V fields) emphasized in this book each have particular approaches, strategies, and tools. The impacts (or effects/results) of each of these on organizational productivity and creativity should be measured. Thus, it should be regularly measured if the activities in enabling new managerial mindsets, facilitating new knowledge management processes, implementing new health (physical, mental, and emotional) processes, adopting new HRM programs and practices, and facilitating appropriate work environments and physical tools have achieved the pre-set objectives (see Chapter 3) in each of these fields, especially in their desired impacts on organizational productivity and creativity.

While the measurement of productivity performance is well developed and relatively easily quantifiable and with many tools available, the measurement of creativity is more difficult and ambiguous. The end result of creativity in an enterprise should be measurable in various types of constructive innovations (be it in competitively advantageous products, processes or business model innovations). The indirect measurement of the levels of positive creativity, such as creative sparks, new ideas, positive mental energy linkages, is much more difficult and not generally agreed upon in theory or practice.

It is outside the scope of this book to provide an in-depth review of this issue but important to emphasize that each enterprise should develop its own objectives and measurements of creativ-

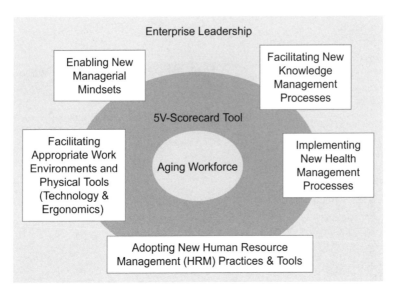

Figure 10.1
The key organizational action fields to manage an aging workforce

ity. In an innovation economy this is becoming crucial for enterprise survival and growth, and with an aging workforce it is evidently very important to stimulate and measure the creativity of such a workforce – see e.g. Davenport, Leibold & Voelpel's work *Strategic Management in the Innovation Economy*.[1]

In Chapter 1, the five key organizational action fields were first illustrated, as now again depicted in Figure 10.1 for purpose of developing the integrated 5V-Scorecard tool.

The Integrated 5V-Scorecard as a Holistic Measurement Tool of the Value-Added of an Aging Workforce

The 5V-framework was first depicted in Figure 1.5 in Chapter 1. The five organizational action fields can now be combined in an integrated 5V-Scorecard, as illustrated in Table 10.1.

Table 10.1
The integrated 5V-Scorecard

		Major Performance Levels to be Measured				
		Productivity		Creativity		
		Efficiency	Effective-ness	New ideas	Mental energy	New processes
Major organizational action fields to increase skills, competencies and capabilities of an aging workforce	Mindsets					
	Knowledge management					
	Health					
	HRM					
	Work environment & physical tools					
	Other topics					

While the above illustration is for a 5V-Scorecard applied to the entire enterprise, it is of course useful and practical to apply it also on the various functional levels of the enterprise, e.g. marketing, production, distribution, logistics and finance (as first depicted in Chapter 4, Table 4.1). The next section illustrates how the various approaches and tools discussed in the previous chapters can be further detailed as part of each organizational action field, and linked to particular measurement tools.

Combining 5V Implementation Tools and Measurement Tools

Table 10.2 illustrates how the 5V implementation tools can be combined with particular 5V-Scorecard measurement tools, with relevant corporate examples.[2]

Table 10.2
Combining 5V implementation tools and measurement tools in managing the aging workforce

Action field	Objective	Implementation tool	Measurement tool	Corporate example
Mindset Change	Positive attitude towards innovation	e-Learning	Rating survey of attitudes	Lufthansa
Knowledge Management	Retention of valuable know-how	Knowledge-depositories	Knowledge audits	Volkswagen
Health & Ergonomics	Physical performance improvements	Workplace reorganization	Workability index; observations	Daimler-Chrysler
HRM(1)	Increase in work flexibility and sharing	People Sharenet	Job satisfaction survey & ratings; trust ratings	Siemens
HRM(2)	Job matching	Software-linked trade-offs	Job turnover; job loyalty	BMW

Table 10.2 demonstrates how important it is to link action field, objective, implementation tool, and measurement tool in managing an aging workforce. This measurement device provides a direct comparison between the type of implementation tool – or intervention action – and its result. The eventual measurement results provide a direct feedback of the relative importance and success rate of particular interventions.

The Dynamics of Utilizing the 5V-Scorecard

It is important that the dynamics of using the 5V-Scorecard are well understood for its successful performance. These are:

- The 5V-Scorecard is a dynamic system with interrelated elements, and a system is only as good as its weakest link. If any one of the five action fields is weak or poorly implemented, it will affect the performance of the other action field interventions. *All planned interventions should be holistically considered and implemented.*

- The relative "soft" issues in the 5V-Scorecard are Mindset Change and Health Management (mental, physical and emotional health), while the relatively "harder" issues are Knowledge Management, even more HRM and Work Environment & Physical Tools. *The harder issues are more amenable to precise structuring and quantification, and one should guard against the possibility of giving greater importance to these due to their relative greater ease of planning, implementation, and measurement.* The softer, more qualitative issues and interventions are often the important platforms for the more quantitative methods and techniques, but they form an essential integrated whole.

- Various types of quantitative and qualitative measurement tools exist, e.g. surveys, audits, rating mechanisms, loyalty measuring techniques, psychometric testing techniques, observations checklists, and quantitatively constructed indices. *A good understanding of these tools, and their appropriate use, is essential to manage the aging workforce.* These techniques are generally well-known and easily available.

Key Pointers of Chapter 10

- The two key enterprise performance indicators that should be measured to determine the effects of managing an aging workforce by way of the 5V-framework are productivity and creativity. While productivity is a well-known concept in measuring practices, creativity is lesser known and requires careful performance measures of e.g. level of new ideas and positive mental energy.

- The 5V-Scorecard is a holistic measurement tool, and integrated scoring frameworks should be constructed for adequate measuring of enterprise efforts in managing the aging workforce. One such framework is a combined implementation tool and measurement tool display.

- The 5V-Scorecard should be understood as a dynamic, action-interrelated concept with inter-linkages and cross-impacts, and should be implemented as such.

- The relatively 'softer', more qualitative issues and interventions are more difficult to devise and implement, but they provide the important platforms for the more "harder" quantitative issues and interventions.

- A good understanding of the various relevant measurement tools, such as surveys, audits, and indices, is essential for effective use of the 5V-Scorecard to manage an aging workforce.

Glossary of Major Terms

5V-framework

The concept of an integrated aging workforce scorecard tool consisting of five critical aging workforce arenas to manage, guide and measure both creativity and productivity of an enterprise's aging workforce. The five key organizational action fields are: enabling new managerial mindsets, facilitating new knowledge management processes, implementing appropriate health (physical, mental, and emotional) processes, adopting relevant Human Resources Management (HRM) programs and practices, and facilitating appropriate work environments and physical tools.

Aging Society

Demographic shifts in the age distribution of the population in especially the developed world indicate that the percentage of the older population (individuals over the age of 55) in society is relatively growing while that of the younger population is relatively decreasing.

Aging Workforce

The aging of the population (or aging society) impacts significantly on the workforce, where the number of aging workers could in the near future rapidly outnumber that of younger workers.

Baby Boomers

This is a popular term used for the group of individuals born in the developed world during the period 1946 to 1964, representing a boom in birthrates after World War II. Those born in 1946 have reached the age of 60 in 2006, with an expected significant wave of retirements starting from 2006 onwards.

Business Model

This is the particular way an enterprise chooses to do business at a certain point in time in such a way that it provides sustainable value and rewards to its various stakeholders, including its shareholders. A business model consists of the particular market needs served, specific types of product and service propositions, particular internal and external value chain configurations, and particular competitive policies and capabilities to profitably sustain itself.

Communities of Practice (CoPs)

These are natural communities – or networks – of people informally (and voluntarily) linked together across traditional organizational and industry boundaries, e.g. by shared expertise, interests and challenges. CoPs can be enabled and guided by enterprise leaders, to mutual benefit of community members and enterprise knowledge and innovation objectives.

Crystallized (or Knowledge-based) Mental Abilities

These are abilities that are maintained or improved over the lifespan. Examples include verbal knowledge and comprehension. (See also: Fluid Mental Abilities).

Deep Smarts

Embedded knowledge, wisdom and expertise that come from experience, insight and foresight. This knowledge is especially experience-based, providing insights drawn from tacit knowledge in conjunction with explicit knowledge, and is also shaped by beliefs and social forces.

Ergonomics

This is the science and practice of integrating human resources (workers) with particular work environments, for optimum long-term productivity and effectiveness of an enterprise (such as worker-pleasant surroundings, lifestyle-enhancing activities, and age-sensitive physical layouts, to mutual benefit of the individual and the enterprise).

Explicit Knowledge

This is knowledge that is known, documented and easily transferable.

Flexible Work Arrangement (or Flexitime)

Non-rigid work arrangements involving a large measure of discretionary behavior concerning when, where and how work is performed, permitting flexibility in work scheduling and the traditional career path.

Fluid (or Process-Based) Mental Abilities

These are abilities that generally show substantial declines during the latter years of individuals' lifespans. Examples include speed of processing, reasoning, and memory encoding and retrieval.

Generation X

This is the generation that was born following the peak of the baby boomers, notably between 1964 and 1981.

Generation Y

Also known as the Ecko Boomers, this is the generation born immediately after Generation X, i.e. since 1981.

Knowledge

This is the capacity for effective action or decision-making in the context of organizational activity. It distinguishes itself from information, which is data that is structured so that it is transferable, but its immediate value depends on the user's ability to interpret and act upon it.

Knowledge-Networked Global Economy

This is the shift of the business world from an industrial economy to one that is knowledge and innovation intensive due to, among others, the advances in communications technology, globalization, networking, new product/service innovation, and increased speed-to-market.

Organizational energy

The dynamic organizational force that reflects the extent to which an enterprise has mobilized its emotional, mental and physical energy potential in pursuit of its goals.

Pre-Boomers

Also known as mature/silent generation, those born before 1946.

Tacit Knowledge

This is knowledge that is 'in people's heads' and that is not documented. It is knowledge that is often not recognized and communicable by employees.

Theory of Constraints (TOC)

is based on the reality that a dynamic system is only as good as its weakest link.

Workability

This is a concept that describes the balance between human resources and work life characteristics. It is basically the sum of factors relating to both an individual's overall health and functional capacities, and the work/value-added requirements that is important for the future performance of the enterprise. In other words, workability is the product of the interaction between work and the resources of the individual – physical, mental and emotional.

Wisdom

This is knowledge and practice that is generated and transmitted at the 'boundaries' between professions, between worlds, between groups and individuals, and between generations. It is knowledge combined with societal and personal values concerning the impacts of actions on various stakeholders. Organizational wisdom is often seen as the virtuous habit of decisions and actions that serve the common good of the enterprise and its various stakeholders.

Notes

Chapter 1

1. Bureau of Labor Statistics, 2001. U.S. Department of Labor, Washington, D.C.

2. Conference Board of Canada, 2001. Performance and Potential, 2000-2001.

3. OECD, 2001. Aging Populations: Economic Issues and Policy Challenges.

4. Pacific Bridge, 2001. "Japan's Labor Market: An Overview."

5. Foster, L., 2005. "Confronting the Global Brain Drain", *KM Review*, Vol. 8, No. 5, November-December, 28-31.

6. Dychtwald, K., Erickson, T.J. and Morison, R., 2006. *Workforce Crisis: How to beat the coming shortage of skills and talent*, Boston: Harvard Business School.

7. Foster, L. *op.cit.*, 29.

8. Foster, L., *op.cit.* 28.

9. Davenport, T.D., Leibold, M. and Voelpel, S., 2006. *Strategic Management in the Innovation Economy*, New York: Publicis/Wiley.

10. See Kuhn, S., 1996. *The Structure of Scientific Revolutions*, Third Edition, Chicago: The University of Chicago Press.

11. Foster, L. *op.cit.*, 30.

12. Foster, L. *op.cit.*, 31.

13. For an elaboration of the concept of a business model, and various definitions and examples of business models, see Davenport, et.al., *op.cit.*, 172-173.

Chapter 2

1. The section on three demographic realities is based on Dychtwald, K., Erickson, T.J., and Morison, R., 2006. *Workforce Crisis: How to beat the coming shortage of skills and talents*, Boston: Harvard Business School Press, 3-6.

2. Adapted from Erickson, T.J., 2005. *Testimony before The U.S. Senate Committee on Health, Education, Labor and Pensions,* May 26, The Concours Group and Age Wave: concoursgroup.com.

3. *Ibid.*

4. *Ibid.*

5. "Older Workers Survey", 2003. *Society for Human Resource Management,* Alexandria, Virginia.

6. Lachnit, C., 2003. "Brave New World", *Workforce,* March, 8.

7. Potter, E.E., 2004. *Testimony before the Special Committee on Aging of the U.S. Senate,* Economic Policy Foundation, September 20.

8. Dychtwald, K., Erickson, T.J. and Morison, R., *op.cit.,* 9-11.

9. Employment Policy Foundation. 2002. "Challenges Facing the American Workplace," *The Seventh Annual Workplace Report.* http://www.epf.org/pubs/laborday-reports/2002.

10. Baker, S., 2002. "The Coming Battle for Immigrants", *Business Week,* August 26.

11. Employment Policy Foundation, *op.cit.*

12. *Ibid.*

13. *Ibid.*

14. This section is adapted from Dychtwald, K., Erickson, T.J. and Morison, *op.cit.* 12-14.

15. IBM Business Consulting Services, 2005. *Addressing the Challenges of an Aging Workforce,* 2.

16. Commission of the European Communities, 2004. "The Stockholm and Barcelona targets: Increasing employment of older workers and delaying the exit from the labour market," *Commission Staff Working Paper,* Brussels, April, 2.

17. *Ibid.*

18. Commission of the European Communities, 2004. "Increasing employment of older workers and delaying the exit from the labour market," *Communication from the Commission to the Council, the European Parliament, The European Economic and Social Committee and the Committee of the Regions,* March 3, 3.

19. Organisation for Economic Co-Operation and Development, 2006. *Live Longer, Work Longer,* Aging and Economic Policies, Paris: OECD.

20. *Ibid.*

21. Jaworski, B., 2005. "Aging Workers, Changing Value", *Journal of Employee Assistance,* 1st Quarter, 23.

22. Foster, L., *op.cit.,* 30-31.

23. DeLong, D.W. 2001. Chemicals Industry Leaders: Are You Ready for the Workforce of the Future? *Changing Workforce Demographics*, Accenture: Institute for Strategic Change.

24. Dychtwald, K., Erickson, T. and Morison, B., 2004. "It's Time to Retire Retirement," *Harvard Business Review*, March, 48-57.

25. IBM Business Consulting Services, *op.cit.*, 4.

26. "Turning Boomers into Boomerangs." *The Economist*, Special Report: The Aging Workforce, February 18th, 2006, 52-54.

27. Jaworski, B., *op.cit.*, 23.

Chapter 3

1. See Dychtwald, K., Erickson, T.J. and Morison, R., 2006. *Workforce Crisis, op.cit.*, chapter 2. This section is adapted from these authors' important work.

2. *Ibid.*

3. "Turning Boomers into Boomerangs", *op.cit.*, 53.

4. *Ibid.*, 54.

5. *Ibid.*, 52.

6. *Ibid.*, 53.

Chapter 4

1. Rizzo, T., 2006. *The Corporate Team and the Theory of Constraints*, http://www.rogo.com/cac/rizzoz.html.

Chapter 5

1. Government of Alberta, 2006. *Safe and Healthy: A Guide to Managing an Aging Workforce*, Alberta Human Resources and Employment.

2. Adapted from Burke, M.E., 2004. *Generational Differences Survey Report*, Society for Human Resource Management.

3. DeLong, D.W., 2005. "Six Mistakes to Avoid When Implementing an Aging Workforce Strategy", *Ideas for Action*, David DeLong & Associates, www.lostknowledge.com.

4. Dychtwald, K., Erickson, T.J. and Morison, R., 2006. *op.cit*, 42-44.

5. *Ibid.*, 49.

6. This section is based on Dychtwald, K., Erickson, T. and Morison, R., 2004. "It's Time to Retire Retirement", *Harvard Business Review*, March, 51-52.

7. *Ibid.*, 52-53.

8. *Ibid.*, 54-55.

9. Erickson, T.J., 2005. *Testimony to the U.S. Senate Committee on Health, Education, Labor and Pensions,* The Concours Group and Age Wave, 9-10.

10. See Bruch, H., Walter, F. and Voelpel, S., 2006. "Charismatic Leadership and Collective Mental Energy: The Mediating Role of Emotional Energy and Job Involvement Climate", Research Workshop Collective Creativity and its Constraints, Critical Management Studies, *66th Annual Academy of Management Conference,* August 11-12, Atlanta, Georgia, USA.

Chapter 6

1. Sternberg, R.J. and Jorden, J., 2005. (Eds.) *Handbook of Wisdom,* New York: Cambridge University Press.

2. See for example:

    – Areldt, M., 2005. How wise people cope with crises and obstacles in life", *ReVision:* Summer, 28(1): 7-19;

    – Baltes, P. and Kunzmann, E., 2004. "The two faces of wisdom: Wisdom as a general theory of knowledge and judgment about excellence in mind vs. wisdom as everyday realization in people and products", *Human Development,* 47: 290-299;

    – Brown, J.S. and Duguid, P., 1991. "Organizational learning and communities-of-practice: Toward a unified view of working, learning, and innovation", *Organization Science,* 2: 40-57;

    – Solomon, J., Marshall, P. and Gardner, H., 2005. "Crossing boundaries to generative wisdom: an analysis of professional work", in Sternberg, R.J. and Jorden, J., 2005. *op.cit.,* 272-296.

3. U.S. General Accounting Office, 2004. U.S. *General Accounting Office Study on Older Workers.* Washington D.C.

4. See Farrell, D. and Greenberg, E., 2005. "The Economic Impact of an Aging Japan", *The McKinsey Quarterly,* May 2005; "Japan 2007 Problem", 2006. *The Economist,* Jan 7th.

5. DeLong, D.W., 2004. *Lost Knowledge: Confronting the Threat of an Aging Workforce,* New York. Oxford University Press, 16-17.

6. *Ibid.*

7. Halverson, R., 2004. "Accessing, Documenting and Communicating Practical Wisdom: The Phronesis of School Leadership Practice", *American Journal of Education,* 111(1): 90-121.

8. DeLong, D.W., 2004. *op.cit.,* 21-22.

9. *Ibid.*, 22-23.

10. This section is adapted from Carter, C., 2004. "When Your Gurus Walk Out the Door", *KM Review*, Vol. 7, Issue 3, July/August, 16-19.

11. See e.g. Nonaka, I. and Takeuchi, H., 1995. *The Knowledge-Creating Company: How Japanese Companies Create the Dynamics of Innovation.* New York: Oxford University Press.

12. See: Hennessy, M., 2006. The retirement age. *CFO*, 22, 3, 42-45.

13. Carter, C., 2004. *op.cit.*

14. Voelpel, S. and Han, Z., 2005. "Managing Knowledge Sharing in China: The Case of Siemens ShareNet", *Journal of Knowledge Management*, 9, 3, 51-63.

15. Adapted from: DeLong, D.W., 2002. *Confronting the Chemical Industry Brain Drain*, Accenture: Institute for Strategic Change, April, 9-11.

16. See Lesser, E., Hausmann, C. and Feuerpeil, S., 2005. Addressing the challenges of an aging workforce: A human capital perspective for companies operating in Europe. *IBM Business Consulting Services* (http://www-1.ibm.com/services/us/bcs/pdf/ge510-4017-aging-work-force.pdf).

17. Delong, D.W., 2002. *Ibid.*, 7-9.

18. This section is based on drawing from the following sources:

    – Leonard, D., 1998. *Wellsprings of Knowledge: building and sustaining the sources of innovation,* Boston: Harvard Business School Press.

    – Leonard, D. and Sensiper, S., 1998. "The Role of Tacit Knowledge in Group Innovation", *California Management Review,* 40(3), 112-132.

    – Leonard, D. and Swap, W.C., 2004. "Deep Smarts", Harvard Business Review, 82(9), 88-97.

    – Leonard, D. and Swap, W.C., 2005a. *When Sparks Fly: Harnessing the Power of Group Creativity,* Boston: Harvard Business School Press.

    – Leonard, D. and Swap, W.C., 2005b. *Deep Smarts: How to Cultivate and Transfer Enduring Business Wisdom,* Boston: Harvard Business School Press.

    – Nonaka, I. and Takeuchi, H., 1995. *The Knowledge-Creating Company, op.cit.*

    – Nonaka, I., Takeuchi, H. and Umemoto, K., 1996. "A Theory of Organizational Knowledge Creation", *International Journal of Technology Management,* 11(7/8), 833-845.

    – Nonaka, I. and Konno, N.,1998. "The Concept of Ba: Building a Foundation of Knowledge Creation", *California Management Review,* 40(3), 40-55.

19. See Nonaka, I., Kohlbacher, F. and Holden, N., 2006. "Aging and Innovation: Recreating and Refining High Quality Tacit Knowledge through Phronetic Leadership", Paper for *2006 Annual Meeting of the Academy of Management (ADM)*, Atlanta: Critical Management Studies Research Workshop – Managing the Aging Workforce: Leadership towards a New Weltanschaung.

20. This section is based on DeLong, D.W., 2004. *Lost Knowledge: Confronting the Threat of an Aging Workforce*. New York: Oxford University Press, 101-118.

21. Lesser, E., Hausmann, C., and Feuerpeil, S., *op.cit.*

22. Lesser, E. 2006. The Maturing Workforce – Managing the Crisis Before It Hits. http://www.learningcircuits.org/2006/January/lesser.htm

23. Adapted from Saint-Onge, H. and Wallace, D., 2003. *Leveraging Communities of Practice for Strategic Advantage*, Boston: Butterworth-Heinemann, 141-207.

24. Adapted from DeLong, D.W., 2004. *Lost Knowledge, op.cit.*, 143-160.

25. *Ibid.*, 217-226.

Chapter 7

1. See: Finnish Institute of Occupational Health, www.enwhp.org/toolbox/pdf/Finland1_Workability_Index.pdf.

2. Bruch, H. and Ghoshal, S., 2003. "Unleashing Organizational Energy", *MIT Sloan Management Review*, Vol. 45, No. 1, Fall, 45-51.

3. Alberta Human Resources and Development, 2006. *Safe and Healthy: A Guide to Managing and Aging Workforce, op.cit.*, 10-17.

4. Dychtwald, K., Erickson, T.J. and Morison, R., 2006. *Workforce Crisis, op.cit.*, 38-40.

5. AARP, 2000. *American Business and Older Employees: A Summary of Findings*.

6. Dychtwald, K., Erickson, T.J. and Morison, R., 2006, *op.cit.*, 39.

7. Eichelkraut, J., 2004. *Testimony before the Special Committee on Aging of the U.S. Senate*, September 14, 3. (Eichelkraut is president of Southwest Airlines Pilots' Association).

8. Wallis, D., 2000. "Act 2.0", *Wired*, May.

9. Kramer, A.F., Fabiani, M. and Colcombe, S.J., 2006. "The Contributions of Cognitive Neuroscience to the Understanding of Behavior and Aging", in Birren A. and Schaie, K.W. (Eds.), *Handbook of the Psychology of Aging*, Sixth Edition, Amsterdam: Elsevier.

10. Baltes, P.B., Staudinger, U.M. and Lindenberger, U., 1999. "Lifespan Psychology: Theory and Application to Intellectual Functioning", *Annual Review of Psychology*, 50, 471-507.

11. See Kramer, A.F., Larrish, J., Webber, T. and Bardell, L., 1999. "Training for Executive Control: Task Coordination Strategies and Aging", in Gopher, D. and Koriat, A. (Eds.), *Attention and Performance* XVII, Cambridge, MA, MIT Press.

12. Adapted from Dolan, K.A., 2006. "Sharp as a Tack", *Forbes*, http://www.forbes.com/free_forbes/2006/0327/072.html.

13. Boulton-Lewis, G., 1997. "Information Processing, Memory, Age and Adult Learning", in Sutherland, P. (ed.), *Adult Learning: A Reader*, London: Kogan Page.

14. Dychtwald, K., Erickson, T.J. and Morison, R., 2006. *op.cit.*, 207-208.

15. Concours Group and Age Wave, 2004. *The New Employee/Employer Equation Survey*, Harris Interactive.

16. European Monitoring Centre on Change (CMCC). 2006. "Inclusion of Aging Workers: Four Company Case Examples", European Foundation for the Improvement of Living and Working Conditions, http://www.emcc.eurofound.eu.int/content/source/eu04009a.html.

17. Wellner, A., 2002, quoted in Goldberg, B., 2005. "How to Become Employer of Choice for the Working Retired", in Beatty, P.T. and Visser, R.M.S. (Eds.), *Thriving on an Aging Workforce: Strategies for Organizational and Systemic Change*, Melbourne: Krieger Publishing Company, 173-176.

18. *Ibid.*

19. Mitchell, K. 2005. Aging Workforce Challenge to Corporate Health and Productivity. *Life & Health Advisor, The Journal for the Financial Services Industry.* (http://www.unumprovident.com/newsroom/publications/Dec% 2005%20Life%20&%20Health%20Advisor%20Mitch ell%20Aging.pdf)

20. Kruger, K., in Burns, 2005. *The Business of Healthcare Innovation*, Cambridge: Cambridge University Press.

21. This section is adapted from AARP, 2006. *Health and Safety Issues in an Aging Workforce*, Washington, DC: AARP Public Policy Institute, 2-3.

22. Adapted from ACSM, 2003. *ACSM's Worksite Health Promotion Manual: A Guide to Building and Sustaining Healthy Worksites*, Champaign, Illinois: American College of Sports Medicine.

23. *Ibid.*, 100-104; 45-60.

24. Bruch, H. and Ghoshal, S., 2003. *op.cit.*, 45-51. Various research projects on the topic 'organizational energy and aging' are in process under leadership of Professor Heike Bruch within the framework

of a research unit at the University of St. Gallen, Switzerland and a company consortium called Organizational Energy Program (OEP).

25. *Ibid.*; see also Bruch. H., Walter F. and Voelpel, S., 2006. "Charismatic Leadership and Collective Mental Energy: The Mediating Role of Emotional Energy and Job Involvement Climate", Research Workshop 'Collective Creativity and its Constraints', Critical Management Studies, *66th Annual Academy of Management Conference*, August 11-12, Atlanta, Georgia, USA.

26. Adapted from: Finnish Institute of Occupational Health, *op.cit.*

27. *Ibid.*

Chapter 8

1. See Görn, A. and Rentzsch, M. (Eds.), 2003. *RESPECT – Solutions for effective Design of Work Life within the Demographical Changes*, http://respect.iccs.ntua.gr.

2. See "Some Firms Strive for Integration", 2003. *Social Agenda*, Vol. 5, April, 11.

3. Adapted from: Alberta Human Resources and Development, 2006. *op.cit.*, 11-15. See this source for a more comprehensive list of discussions on the topic.

4. See ACSM, 2003. *op.cit.*, 103-104.

5. See Amditis, A., et.al. 2003. in Strasser, H., Kluth, K., Rausch, H. and Bubb, H. (Eds.), *Dealing with the Problems of an Elderly Workforce – The RESPECT Approach*, Stuttgart: Ergonomia Verlag, 881-884.

6. See a) R.A. Malatest & Associates Ltd., 2003. The Aging Workforce and Human Resources Development Implications, A Report prepared for The Alliance of Sector Councils. (http://www.cpsc-ccsp.ca/PDFS/Aging%20Workforce%20Final%20Report.pdf); b) Good Practice in the Recruitment and Retention of Older Workers: Summary. 2001. Produced by the Department for Work and Pensions. (www.agepositive.gov.uk/complogos/ASHDOWNGoodPracticeSummary.doc).

7. Adapted from IBM Consulting Services, 2005. *Addressing the Challenges of an Aging Workforce: A human capital perspective for companies operating in Europe*, Somers, NY: IBM Global Services.

8. Stoney, C. and Roberts, M., 2003. "The Case for Older Workers at Tesco: An examination of attitudes, assumptions and attributes," Carleton University School of Public Policy and Administration, *Working Paper, No. 53*. June. http://www/Carleton.ca/spa/Publication/WP%2053%20Stoney.pdf.

9. Morris, M. and Viswanath V., 2000. "Age differences in technology adoption decisions: Implications for a changing workforce," *Personnel Psychology*, Vol. 53, No. 2, July, 375-403.

10. This section is adapted from: Mosner, E., Speizle, C. and Emerman, J., 2003. *The Convergence of the Aging Workforce and Accessible Technology: The Implications for Commerce*, Business and Policy, Microsoft Corporation and Age Light Marketing Consultancy, July, 9-15.

11. Based on Orlov, L.M., 2004. "Reversing the Aging Workforce Crisis", *Best Practices*, Cambridge, MA: Forrester Research Inc., 1-2, with focus on IBM's w3 Intranet applications.

12. *Ibid.*, 3.

Chapter 9

1. Erickson, T.J., 2005. T*estimony before the U.S. Senate Committee on Health, Education, Labor and Pensions*, Washington DC: The Concours Group and Age Wave, 2-4.

2. Bruch, H., Walter, F. and Voelpel, S., 2006. "Charismatic Leadership and Collective Mental Energy: The Mediating Role of Emotional Energy and Job Involvement Climate", Research Workshop 'Collective Creativity and its Constraints', Critical Management Studies, *66th Annual Academy of Management Conference*, August 11-12, Atlanta, Georgia, USA.

3. Erickson, T.J., 2005. *op.cit.*, 11.

4. The Economist, 2006. *Turning Boomers into Boomerangs*, Special Report: The Aging Workforce, February 18th, 52.

5. European Monitoring Centre on Change, 2006. *The Workplace of the Future – Managing the Challenge of an Aging Workforce*, Paris: European Foundation for the Improvement of Living and Working Conditions, http://www.emcc.eurofound.eu.int/print/source/eu04014a. html, 2-3.

6. Goldberg, B., 2005. "How to Become Employer of Choice for the Working Retired", in Beatty, P.T. and Visser, R.M.S. (Eds.), *Thriving on an Aging Workforce: Strategies for Organizational and Systemic Change*, Melbourne: Krieger Publishing Company, 173-176.

7. Lesser, E., Hausmann, C. and Feuerpeil, S., 2005. Addressing the challenges of an aging workforce: A human capital perspective for companies operating in Europe. *IBM Business Consulting Services*. (http://www-1.ibm.com/services/us/bcs/pdf/ge510-4017-aging-workforce.pdf).

8. Hennessy, M., 2006. The retirement age. *CFO*, 22, 3, 42-45

9. American Association of Retired Persons (AARP), 2006. (http://www.aarp.org/money/careers/employerresourcecenter/bestpractices/a2004-12-17-flexiblework.html).

10. DeLong, D.W., 2004. *Lost Knowledge: Confronting the Threat of an Aging Workforce, op.cit.,* 57-59.

11. *Ibid.,* 66.

12. *Ibid.,* 77-79.

13. Lesser, E., Hausmann, C. and Feuerpeil, S., 2005. *op.cit.*

14. This section is predominantly based on: Dychtwald, K., Erickson, T.J. and Morison, R., 2006. *Workforce Crisis; How to Beat the Coming Shortage of Skills and Talents,* Boston, Harvard Business School Press, 135-178.

15. Shutan, B., 2004. "Feeling Right at Home: Home Depot Dangles a Broad Benefits Package to Woo Older Workers", http://www.agewave.com/media_maddy/press 11_04.html.

16. Dychtwald, K., Erickson, T.J. and Morison, R., 2006. *op.cit.*182.

17. *Ibid,* 189-194.

18. DeLong, D.W., 2006. "The Paradox of the 'Working Retired' – Identifying Barriers to Increased Labor Force Participation by Older Workers in the U.S.", *Academy of Management CMS Research Workshop: Managing the Aging Workforce – Leadership towards a New Weltanschaung.* Atlanta: August 11, 17-18.

19. *Ibid.,* 6.

Chapter 10

1. Davenport, T., Leibold, M. and Voelpel, S., 2006. *Strategic Management in the Innovation Economy: Strategy Approaches and Tools for Dynamic Innovation Capabilities,* New York: John Wiley & Sons/Publicis.

2. Adapted from Voelpel, S. and Streb, C., 2006. "Wettbewerbsfähigkeit im Demographischen Wandel: Vom Risiko zur Chance", *Personalwirtschaft,* Vol. 33, No. 8, 24-27.

Index

Davenport, Thomas H.; Probst,
Gilbert J.B. (Editors)

Knowledge Management Case Book

Best Practises

*With a Foreword by Dr. Heinrich von Pierer,
former President and CEO of Siemens AG*

2nd revised and enlarged edition, 2002,
336 pages, 79 illustrations, 4 tables, hardcover
ISBN-10: 3-89578-181-9
ISBN-13: 978-3-89578-181-0
€ 39.90 / sFr 64.00 / £ 29.95 / US $ 60.00

This book provides a perspective on knowledge management at Siemens –
according to an international benchmarking (MAKE) one of the 'top ten
KM companies worldwide' – by presenting the reader with the best of the
corporation's practical applications and experiences. Davenport and Probst
bring together instructive case studies from different areas that reflect the
rich insights gained from years of experience in practising knowledge management.

For the second edition, the Knowledge Management Case Book has been
updated and enlarged with new cases and add-ons. Thus it once again provides concrete examples of the way Siemens is fostering, promoting and
optimizing knowledge utilization. The individual case studies included are
also a valuable source of ideas for efficient, targeted knowledge management.

Presenting applications from very different areas, this practice-orientated
book is really outstanding in the broad field of KM literature.

Contents

Siemens Knowledge Journey · Knowledge Strategy · Knowledge Transfer ·
Communities of Practice · Added value of Knowledge Management ·
Learning and Knowledge Management · Visualizing more of the Value
Creation · Rethinking KM · Case-writing as a Knowledge Management
and organizational Learning Tool.

Lucks, Kai (Editor)

Transatlantic Mergers and Acquisitions

Opportunities and Pitfalls in
German-American Partnerships

2005, 480 pages, 107 illustrations, hardcover
ISBN-10: 3-89578-262-9
ISBN-13: 978-3-89578-262-6
€ 88.00 / sFr 141.00 / £ 65.00 / US $ 120.00

This book is intended to show ways to successful cooperation. Going beyond M&A, it demonstrates how economical ties and personal behaviour can positively influence our international relations. The value to M&A professionals will be generated through better understanding the views from the other side of the Atlantic, through new M&A insights from other industries and from experts working in consulting and finance. Thus, it is also of high value to all those working on partnerships between the USA or Germany and any other country.

The book deals with many different aspects, starting from overall strategies, and ending up with lessons learnt from the special cases. Reflecting behavioural, economic or legal aspects, there are articles showing one side only to work out country or industry specifics and others comparing the nationally different systems and surroundings.

The authors of the book are executives with specific experiences in M&A, high-level professionals in the M&A area, experienced international M&A managers and top consultants in different areas of M&A – each from both sides of the Atlantic.

Contents

Markets and structures: M&A in Germany · Success Factors in Transatlantic M&A · Markets and Trends from German and US Perspectives.

Experiences from Different Industries: Automotive · Banking & Finance · Chemical, Pharmaceutical & Healthcare · Consumer · Food · Power Generation & Electronics · Information & Communication · Logistics & Transportation · Materials · Media · Private Equity Investments in Various Industries.

Professional & Functional Contributions: Communications in Transatlantic M&A · Leadership, Strategy and Structure · Corporate Governance · Legal & Tax Conditions · Antitrust Control · Financial & Accounting · Patents & Technology · Culture, Communications & Personnel.

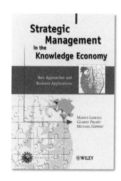

Leibold, Marius; Probst, Gilbert J.B.;
Gibbert, Michael

Strategic Management in the Knowledge Economy

New Approaches and Business Applications

2nd updated edition, 2005, 355 pages, hardcover
ISBN-10: 3-89578-257-2
ISBN-13: 978-3-89578-257-2
€ 39.90 / sFr 64.00 / £ 29.95 / US $ 60.00

Due to the dramatic shifts in the knowledge economy, this book provides a significant departure from traditional strategic management concepts and practice. Designed for both advanced students and business managers, it presents a unique combination of new strategic management theory, carefully selected strategic management articles by prominent scholars such as Gary Hamel, Michael Porter, Peter Senge, and real-world case studies.

On top of this, the authors link powerful new benchmarks in strategic management thinking, including the concepts of Socio-Cultural Network Dynamics, Systemic Scorecards, and Customer Knowledge Management with practical business challenges and solutions of blue-chip companies with a superior performance (Lafite-Rothschild, Who's Who, Holcim, BRL Hardy, Kuoni BTI, Deutsche Bank, Unisys, Novartis).

Contents

Fundamental impacts of the global knowledge economy on strategic management · Traditional strategic management approaches, and their deficencies · New mindset: systemic strategic management · Frameworks for systemic strategic management · Strategic management tools for the knowledge economy · Managing the new strategic leadership challenges.

Davenport, Thomas H.; Leibold, Marius;
Voelpel, Sven

Strategic Management in the Innovation Economy

Strategy Approaches and Tools for
Dynamic Innovation Capabilities

2006, 441 pages, 38 illustrations, hardcover
ISBN-10: 3-89578-263-7
ISBN-13: 978-3-89578-263-3
€ 32.90 / sFr 53.00 / £ 24.95 / US $ 55.00

*"Innovation is the key challenge for business today, and this book offers
a wonderfully insightful new strategic approach. Great analysis and an
up-to-date selection of readings and cases."*

Paul Adler, University of Southern California

*"This is a unique book on strategy and strategizing in the innovation
economy. Leaders and Executives in all organizations need to pay close
attention to this book. This is the new direction for strategy in our 21st
century, and Davenport, Leibold and Voelpel's book is the first available
source."*

Nitin Nohria, Harvard Business School

*"This book provides a new platform for strategic management approaches
and tools, and I trust it will find a particular place in the field of strategic
management for innovation, both in business practice and education."*

Heinrich v. Pierer, former CEO of Siemens AG

*"Based on wide ranging international inputs, the authors offer a superb
strategic tool-kit. They take us beyond the Balanced Scorecard to their
own Poised Scorecard, more flexible, multi-purposed and practical, and
show us the potential of today's networked business eco-systems."*

JC Spender, Leeds University Business School